The Complete
FLOWER CRAFT
Book

THE COMPLETE
FLOWER CRAFT
BOOK

SUSAN CONDER SUE PHILLIPS
PAMELA WESTLAND

NORTH LIGHT BOOKS

Cincinnati, Ohio

ACKNOWLEDGMENTS:

The publishers would like to thank the following photographers and artists for their kind permission to reproduce their work:

PHOTOGRAPHS

C Crofton 38, 97(R), 114, 116, 117, 135, 136, 137

D Garcia 14, 16, 17, 30, 51(T), 62, 64, 65, 139, 140, 141

N Hargreaves 110

A Hodgeson 112, 113

R McMahon 6, 7, 8, 11 12, 13, 23, 24, 25, 32, 33, 40, 41, 42, 44, 45, 53, 54, 55, 56, 57, 58, 60(R), 61, 79(B), 92, 94, 95, 97(L), 98, 100, 101, 102, 103, 104, 105, 107, 108(R), 109, 118, 119, 120, 121, 134

M Smallcombe 9, 10, 18, 20, 21, 22, 27, 28, 29, 34, 36, 37, 46, 48, 49, 50, 51(B), 66, 68, 69, 70, 71, 72, 73, 74, 75, 76, 78, 79(T), 81, 82(R), 83, 84, 85, 86, 87, 89, 90(R), 91, 96, 122, 124, 125, 126, 128, 129, 130, 132, 133

ARTWORK

W Giles 19, 44, 47

J Pickering 26, 31, 32, 59, 60, 63, 67, 132(L)

S Pond 35, 39, 72(L), 82(L), 90(L), 93, 108(L)

This compilation first published in Great Britain in 1993
by Hamlyn, an imprint of Reed Consumer Books Limited,
Michelin House, 81 Fulham Road, London SW3 6RB
and Auckland, Melbourne, Singapore and Toronto

© This compilation Reed International Books Limited 1993

First published in the United States by North Light Books
an imprint of F&W Publications, Inc.
1507 Dana Avenue, Cincinnati, Ohio 45207
1-800-289-0963

The material in this book was originally published in 1988
by Orbis Publishing Limited

© Orbis Publishing Limited 1988

ISBN 0-89134-539-6

Produced by Mandarin Offset
Printed and bound in Hong Kong

GLOSSARY

aerosol = spray can
attic = loft
autumn = fall
bedside table = nightstand
biscuit = cookie
builder's merchant = hardware store/lumber yard
caster sugar = superfine sugar
ceiling rose = ceiling medallion
chemist = drug store/druggist
chilli = chili pepper
cloakroom = closet
cotton wool = cotton ball
cupboard = closet or cabinet
curtain rail = drape rail
dustbin liner = trash can liner
electric socket = electric outlet
flat = apartment
greengrocer = fruit and vegetable store
jam = jelly
jelly = jello
kitchen paper = paper towel
kitchen storage unit = kitchen cabinet
organza = organdy
pudding = dessert
rubber band = elastic band
saucepan = pan or skillet
scone = biscuit
secondhand shop = thriftstore
tap = faucet
tin = can
tinned goods = canned goods
wire cutters = pliers

imperial liquid measures
16 fl oz = approximately
1 American pint (2 cups)

CONTENTS

INTRODUCTION

This is both a practical handbook and a source of stylish information. It takes a look at some of the many and varied longlasting displays which can be made with dried and silk flowers, and at ways of combining fresh and artificial flowers, fruit, berries and nuts. There are arrangements of all sizes; some are very simple to make, while others more complicated and time-consuming. It also gives instructions for some of the surprisingly large number of other items which can be made with flowers, from scented candles, pot pourri and a pressed flower sampler, to floral bath oil and a selection of edible gifts.

The dried flower arrangements range from a dramatic dried-flower ball to hang over a stairwell to a delicate posy with a lace collar, and from a horseshoe of flowers, a good luck token for a bride to carry instead of a traditional bouquet, to an extremely lifelike but totally troublefree Japanese bonsai. There's also information on air drying your own flowers.

The techniques for making some of your own silk flowers are also explained, but the arrangements, from a simple elegant display to a totally fantastic one to serve as a centrepiece for a theme party, can all be made with shop-bought blooms.

The 'Mixed Medleys' are different again – a fascinating selection of some of the striking and unusual arrangements which can be made by combin-

Exciting projects of all shapes and sizes. *Opposite*, a large hanging basket contains a display of fresh and dried flowers. *Left,* an elegant little posy with a lace collar and, *below,* a sampler with an intricate design made with pressed flowers

ing materials of varying sorts, fresh cut flowers with pot plants, dried flowers with fresh blooms and even with totally artificial fruit, nuts and berries.

There is no need to follow all the details of these arrangements slavishly if you don't want to. Meticulous copying is not the idea. They are there as an inspiration, and to explain the basic principles of making various types of display. Throughout the book there are suggestions for alternative flowers, foliage, containers and colour schemes which can be used. Take them as a starting point from which to develop your own style and make displays using your favourite flowers, in your favourite colours, to suit your home.

Clear step-by-step photographs make all the projects easy to follow, and hint panels provide extra information on complicated techniques. Throughout the book there are notes on how to care for both displays and crafted items.

PERFECTLY PRESERVED

Dried flowers are versatile and good tempered, their dusty image a thing of the past. Far from being a poor substitute for fresh flowers, they have a charming informality all their own

The choice of dried flowers in shops and garden centres today is greater than it has ever been before, with a wide selection of flowers, foliage and seed pods available in natural colours, bleached and dyed hues. If you are lucky enough to have a garden, you can grow your own flowers for air drying (see pages 10-13 for a list of plant materials suitable for air drying and for instructions). Country walks can yield lovely dried flowers and seed pods of common weeds, such as cow parsley and ground elder, while urban wasteland is a good hunting ground for buddleia and rose bay willow herb.

Dried flowers are both economic and long-lasting. An arrangement will give pleasure for many months and when you tire of it it can be revamped with fresh flowers or taken apart and stored for future use, for dried flowers can be used again and again. In fact, making an arrangement with dried flowers is good practice for beginners as no amount of handling will cause them to wilt or die.

T hree ways with dried flowers. The sewing basket (*opposite*) contains a charming display of cottage garden flowers. *Left*: a life-like bonsai made of dried moss and a gnarled branch, and, (*below*), a dried-flower horseshoe for a bride

Generally speaking, the stems of dried flowers, stripped of their thorns and most of their leaves, add little to the beauty of an arrangement, particularly since some of the shorter stems need to be mounted on stub wires and bound with gutta-percha tape. For this reason, it is the stems which determine one of the general principles of dried flower arranging. If you look closely at any attractive display, you will see that the flowers are placed so closely together (but not so close that they squash or damage each other) that the stems are invisible.

When not in use, store your dried flowers in an airy, dust-free place, with a warm, even temperature and out of direct sunlight. Lidded cardboard boxes – shoe boxes for small items and the florists' delivery boxes for larger ones – are ideal. Make a few holes in the boxes for the air to circulate freely. Wrap flowers loosely in generous quantities of tissue paper, making sure you give adequate support to large flower-heads. Never store dried flowers in plastic bags.

In this chapter we have dried flower displays, both large and small, and of varying standards of difficulty, for almost every room in the house, from a dramatic hanging ball for a hall to a tiny posy with a lace collar, ideal for a bedside table. Finally, a word of warning, do not put a dried flower arrangement in a bathroom. The atmosphere is too hot and steamy.

AIR DRYING
TECHNIQUES

Allowing flowers and other plant materials to dry out in the air is the easiest and most popular method of preserving them.

Although the principle of air drying remains the same whatever plant materials you use, the basic method can be adapted to suit individual foliage varieties.

PICKING PERFECT SPECIMENS

Select flowers that are in good condition, undamaged by insects or the weather. Pick them on a dry day, after the morning dew has dried and before the sun is at its hottest. Alternatively, pick them shortly before the evening dew has begun to form. If you do not have a garden, select perfect specimens from the florist.

Choose your drying area with similar care: it must be dry, cool – but no less than 10°C (50°F), well ventilated and the air should circulate freely; airing cupboards, attics, and garages usually meet all these criteria – modern kitchens tend to be too hot and damp. Avoid hanging the flowers in direct sunlight as this causes the colours to fade, and avoid excess damp as this encourages mould.

To achieve strong, natural colours in the dried material, it is important to make the drying period as short as possible.

The time taken for flowers and foliage to dry completely depends on their density and size, the temperature, humidity and amount of air movement in the drying environment. The process usually takes about four to ten days. The plant material is ready when it feels crisp and papery and rustles gently; seedheads should rattle.

THE HANGING METHOD

This method – hanging flowers in bunches, with their heads pointing downwards – is used for the widest range of flowers, including everlasting flowers – members of the *Compositae* family – long-stemmed delphiniums, astilbe, lavenders, pink heathers, golden rod, mimosa and roses.

Learn the simple secrets of drying fresh flowers and seedheads and become your own supplier of dried display material

SUITABLE MATERIALS FOR AIR DRYING

Acanthus, achillea (yarrow), African daisy, allium, anaphalis, antirrhinum, astilbe, bluebell, Chinese lantern, clary, cornflower, delphinium, dock, globe thistle, golden rod, gypsophila, heather, hollyhock, hydrangea, iris, lady's mantle, larkspur, lavender, mimosa, molucella, nigella, poppy, sea holly, shepherd's purse, tansy, teasel, thistle, and thrift

MOISTURE TESTS

If you are not sure whether your flowers are completely dry, try these tests.

• Always test a flower in more than one place. Often the petals dry before the flower centre.

• Place a suspect flower or a few leaves in a small air-tight jar. Leave for a day or two. If condensation appears, the flowers and foliage need to be dried a little more.

• Often the 'neck' of the flower dries out last. Check that a bunch is dry by standing a sample flower upright in a container for 24-48 hours. The head will droop if the plant is not completely dry.

Before drying, check to make sure that the stems are in good condition and will not break. Remove any damaged material, thorns and the lower leaves from the stems, leaving them bare at the point where they are to be tied, as trapped leaves may go mouldy and rot.

Group the flowers in several bunches, staggering the levels of the heads. Using raffia, thick string or wide tape, tie the bare lower stems together fairly tightly with a slip-knot that can be tightened as the stems dry and contract. Make a loop from which to hang the stem ends. Alternatively, fasten bunches together with an elastic band and make an 'S' shaped hook with a stub wire from which to hang the bunch. Spread out the flowers and leaves to ensure the air can circulate. Hang the bunches from hooks or an indoor clothes line. Make sure they are well spaced.

To prevent the heads of short-stemmed flowers, such as multiflora roses, from drooping, wire the stems underneath the flowerheads before drying and group into bunches of about ten stems. Tie the stems together securely near the bottom and ease the wired stems outwards gently so that none of the flowerheads touch. Once dry, the supporting wire stems can be successfully disguised with green gutta-percha tape.

1 Thick woody-stemmed plants with tiny flowers, such as golden rod, are particularly suitable for air drying and need little special treatment. Detach any damaged flowerheads or imperfect upper leaves. Remove the lower foliage from the stems as they tend to retain moisture that may impede the drying process. They may cause the plant stem to rot if left on the stem.

2 Group the stems into bunches of four. Secure with an elastic band about 5cm (2in) from the stem ends. Bind the ends with a piece of twine, leaving its ends free to attach to a pole for drying. Sometimes goden rod droops after hanging for a few days. You can counteract this by standing the bunch upright half way through the drying procedure.

3 Repeat the same basic method for hollow-stemmed plants such as larkspur. Trim any excess greenery from the stems of one bunch of larkspur, as before, to guard against mould. Cut the flower stems to a length of 20cm (8in). Group the flowers into bunches of four or five stems. If any of the stems appears particularly weak, wire it for extra strength.

4 Secure with an elastic band. Spread out the stems so that they don't touch one another. Bend a length of thick gauge stub wire into an 'S' shape. Attach one end of this hook to the elastic band and use the other to hang the bunch.

Any flowers with heavy heads, such as onion flowers and large protea flowers, should be dried individually with the heads supported by a wire rack. Allow the stems to dangle freely.

DRYING FLAT

Grasses and seedheads that are supported on slender stems should be dried flat. Most mosses, bamboos, fungi and twigs also can be dried this way. Although leaves keep their colour well by this method, they tend to shrivel.

Lay a single layer of the plant material on an absorbent surface. Arrange the material so that none of it is touching and the air can circulate. Turn the stems over occasionally to ensure they dry out evenly.

STANDING – WET OR DRY

The best way to dry small, fragile flowers such as yarrow, fennel and dainty grasses is by putting their stems into florist's dry foam or standing them in a container large enough to allow the free circulation of air.

Paradoxically, some flowers dry most successfully if they are left standing in water; this is the best method of preserving the colour and shape of hydrangea flowerheads, small paeonies, and pom-pom dahlias. Stand the stems in 2.5-5cm (1-2in) of water and leave for two to three weeks. At first, the stems absorb some of the water. However, as the water evaporates, so does the moisture in the plant material until eventually it dries out entirely.

DRYING SEEDHEADS

It is important to pick seedheads for drying when they are fully formed but still green, just as the flower petals have fallen. Although most seedheads can be dried using the basic hanging procedure, some have special drying requirements. For example, Chinese lanterns need to be dried in an upright position, otherwise their lanterns may not hang as they do when fresh.

5 This method involves wiring the flowerheads before drying them and is suited to heavy-headed blooms, such as roses, where the dried stems may be unable to support the weight of the flowerhead. Select good quality, undamaged flowers. Using a pair of scissors, carefully remove all the thorns and leaves from the stems. Trim them to a length of 20cm (8in).

6 Wire each flower stem to hold the flowerheads in position while drying. Use a 20cm (8in) medium gauge stub wire to pierce the calyx, push the wire through the flower base and bend it over 2.5cm (1in) from the top to form a 'U' shape. Pull this back into the calyx. Wind the wire once under the flowerhead and wrap the remainder of the wire loosely around the stem.

7 Bunch the roses together. Large, full flowerheads, such as rose blooms, should not touch while drying, so arrange the heads so that they are on different levels. If the flowers are not staggered, the air will not be able to circulate freely around them as they are drying and they could rot. Secure the stem ends together with an elastic band.

8 Make an 'S' shape from thick gauge stub wire and attach this to the elastic band securing the roses. Erect a bamboo pole or a washing line in a cool, well-ventilated place and attach the roses to it. If you are hanging several bunches at one time, make sure that they do not touch. Leave the material until it is completely dry before arranging.

EASY ELEGANCE

A dried flower arrangement certainly gives value for time and money. What's marvellous about this display is that it's so adaptable. It looks delightful in the bedroom, as shown here, but would be equally at home in a living room, dining room or an entrance hall.

BEST FOR BEGINNERS

Cone-shaped displays like this one are among the simplest to create. There is no front or back to worry about, nor any problem with getting the balance right providing you keep turning the display as you go along. In addition, your display can be made as large or as small as you like.

Once you have roughly worked out the diameter, centre and height of the arrangement, then it is easy to build up the flowers, foliage and grasses into an evenly dense structure.

CHOOSING THE FLOWERS

Delicacy is the theme of this arrangement, and even though the range of flowers is limited, dried rosebuds, gypsophila and glixia combine to create a rich texture and subtle contrast in colour and form.

All three flowers can be bought ready-dried, but rosebuds and gypsophila air-dry so easily that you might well prefer to prepare your own. Even if bought fresh from a florist, you'll find that drying the flowers yourself keeps costs down. The pale pink rosebuds have a uniquely old-fashioned charm, and though they are relatively expensive, you get double value for money as the dried leaves can be reassembled and put to good use in the display. Wholesalers stock a range of dried pink rosebuds – some with a bluish tone, others with a hint of yellow. It does not matter which you choose providing you adjust the other flower colours in the display accordingly.

TRY SOMETHING DYED

For a rosebud effect on a budget, you could use *Carthamus tinctorius*, or safflower – a hardy annual whose plump green flower buds closely resemble roses. And luckily, the dried leaves of this unusual annual can also be used in the display.

Tiny pink glixia are available in a wide range of dyed colours – some more realistic than others! Here, a soft pink has been chosen, but in a slightly paler tone to reinforce the pink of the rosebuds.

Each dainty glixia flower looks like a miniature star, but used singly, they tend to disappear into the background. To give them more impact, florists often wire glixia flowerheads into tight bunches. (For details on wiring dried flowers, see the step-by-step instructions on page 17.) Pink-dyed broom bloom, or nipplewort, would give a very similar effect if broken into tiny florets and wired into bunches.

Gypsophila, or baby's breath, is so well known it needs no description, though it is more often seen in its

A bedside table is a charming location for flowers, especially in a guest bedroom. Dried flowers are a good idea here, as they last from one guest's visit to the next. Before a guest arrives, check the display for any fallen petals or seed pods

white-flowered form than the creamy beige used here. However, if you prefer to use white gypsophila for this arrangement, it will look every bit as good.

GYPSOPHILA AND GRASSES

When dividing the gypsophila into pieces, remember that the further the stems are from the flower, the stronger they will be. Tiny sprigs of gypsophila are wired together to form florets, as with the glixia, but if you use stems 15cm (6in) long, as here, you shouldn't need to use wire.

Test a piece before starting, and if it bends or snaps when inserted into the foam block try a slightly longer, thicker stem – it is much easier to insert the stem deeper into the foam than it is to wire up short stems.

Florets of dried cow parsley could be used instead of gypsophila – a free bonus if you live in the country. Colours are limited to the creamy white and green range, depending on when you pick and dry the flowerheads, but they will fit in well with virtually any colour scheme.

The grasses, avena (feathery) and phalaris (dense) used in this display

DRIED FLOWER CARE

- Pack surplus dried flowers in sealed cardboard boxes – ask your local florist for old flower boxes.
- Make sure that the flowers, including the stems, are completely dry before packing them away.
- Pack carefully ensuring there is not too much pressure on the flower-heads.
- Wrap fragile petalled bunches, such as roses, in tissue paper. Large flowerheads such as paeony or hydrangea should be individually wrapped in tissue paper.
- Never store air-dried and glycerine-dried material in the same box.
- Never pack away dried flowers in plastic wrappings.
- Label boxes and keep cool and dry in a well-ventilated room.

are available from florists but also grow in the garden and on wasteland. Other alternatives you might like to use are meadow foxtail, cocksfoot grass, barley, holcus, wheat, ferns, ribwort, cat's tail or timothy. If picking your own grasses from the garden, woodland or meadow, you may not recognise these varieties, so just go by looks and choose any attractive greeny-grey grasses, one with a dense appearance, the other more delicate and feathery. Some grasses will cut your hand, so wear leather or gardening gloves when picking. Do remember, though, that some plants are protected by law and the flowers, roots, seeds or foliage cannot be taken from them. Local authorities and libraries can supply lists of the protected species in your area.

CHOOSING THE CONTAINER
Here, a crisp white china pedestal vase has been chosen to display the flowers. This type of vase is worth investing in, as it can be used for many other types of flower display. Vases in this style are also available in plastic, but as well as tending to wobble, they never really lose their plastic feel. On the other hand, a creamy alabaster pedestal vase or a Victorian fruit stand would be exquisite. Dried flowers generally have a rustic look so, if you buy a china container specially for a dried flower arrangement, go for a matt or 'eggshell' finish rather than one that is very glossy. Likewise, it is generally better to choose 'soft' designs and patterns rather than sharply defined ones.

The formality of this display is partly due to the elegant shape of the pedestal vase, but you could equally well use a flat-bottomed bowl instead. Make sure, however, that it is a round one, as it is difficult to build up a cone-shaped display in an oval container.

Whatever container you use, it is important to make sure the edge of the cone arrangement is well-filled out all round, and that the flowers and grasses cover the rim.

1 20 dried pink rosebuds
2 1 large bunch of creamy-beige gypsophila
3 2 bunches of pink glixia
4 2 bunches of avena grass
5 2 bunches of phalaris grass
6 pedestal vase, preferably china
7 block of florist's foam
8 adhesive clay
9 florist's tape
10 stub wire
11 prong
12 floristry scissors
13 kitchen knife

SIX STEPS
TO AN ELEGANT PEDESTAL VASE DISPLAY

1 Measure, cut, shape and fix a foam block to the container securely, running florist's tape right across the top, and again at right angles to form a cross. Break off small bunches of gypsophila and push the stems into the side of the foam block, angled slightly downwards. Work round the edge of the container, making a fairly thick band all the way round.

2 Fix the display's height by inserting a 15cm (6in) bunch of gypsophila in the top centre of the foam, where the strips of tape meet. Insert bunches of gypsophila along both tapes, to divide the foam into quarters. Fill each one with about six bunches of gypsophila. Keep turning the vase as you work, making sure that the bunches are evenly thick.

3 Shorten the avena stems to 7.5cm (3in) from below the seed heads. Insert the stems singly into the foam; they are strong enough not to need wiring. Beginning in the centre of the arrangement, add more stems until the avena is roughly the same height as the gypsophila. Work round the edge, then fill in the middle, as with the gypsophila.

4 Shorten the phalaris stems below the heads to 15cm (6in) long. Insert bunches of four into the foam at random. Add some singly, for variety. Shorten the rose stems to 10cm (4in) below the buds, reserving the cut-off stems and leaves. Place one rose in the centre top. Take the rest and place them singly round the edge of the vase and to fill in any spaces in the middle.

5 Strip the rose leaves from the stems. Wire 20 bunches of two, three and four leaves together. Bend a 15cm (6in) wire tightly round the leaf stalks, cut the wire stem to 10cm (4in) and insert the bunches randomly in the foam. By varying the number of leaflets per bunch a more natural look is achieved. Tight bunches have more impact than single leaves.

6 Lastly, divide the pink glixias into bunches of 20, then cut the stems to a length of 5cm (2in) below the tiny heads. Wire the flowers together, using the same method as for the rose leaves. Randomly insert the bunches, turning the vase to ensure even distribution. Make any final adjustments needed to give a cone-shaped display.

STAIRWAY
SPLENDOUR

Flower-packed hanging balls form a decorative feature in many fashionable restaurants and interior design shops. Here we show you how to bring this stylish display to a home setting. A dried-flower ball display does take time to make, which is partly why they are so expensive to buy, but they're not difficult to construct once you have mastered the basic technique.

A dried-flower hanging ball is, by its nature, symmetrical. However, you can achieve a variety of different looks by adjusting the length of the flower stems. Use short-stemmed flowers for a tight covering of flowers or longer stems for a loosely packed and more informal silhouette.

For a special event, such as a wedding, a large flower ball can make a perfect decoration for the church or reception room. A smaller ball on a silk ribbon could serve as an attractive bridesmaid's posy for a young girl. For a festive Christmas hanging ball, you can change the colour scheme of the dried material to red and green and hang it up with a length of silky red or gold ribbon.

OBTAINING FOAM BASES
Dry florist's foam balls are available in two standard sizes, large and small. To look effective, they must be generously full, which takes a large amount of dried flowers. If you are on a tight budget, then pack the foam with an inexpensive but brightly coloured filler, such as perennial statice or hydrangea. If you grow pampas grass, use this as filler, dividing the huge plumes into smaller sprigs and wiring them up into clusters.

When building up the flower ball, it is important to bear in mind that it will be viewed from a distance. For maximum impact, choose dried material with strong variations in texture and

A dried-flower ball made from sea lavender, hydrangea, white and yellow achillea, phalaris, cockscomb, carthamus, helipterum, dill, broom bloom and Spanish moss

bold colours. Delicate plant material should be added in groups or clusters of a single type, while solid, composite flowerheads, such as yarrow and cockscomb, are used whole. The flowers are built up evenly over the entire surface, rather than starting in one area and spreading outwards. For convenience, it is best to hang the foam ball above a work surface for as it becomes fuller it gets more difficult to handle. This also allows you to rotate the ball gently during the construction process and so produce a round, evenly covered arrangement. But most of all, it is important to be able to view the display from below because its intended location is well above people's eye level.

Choosing the flowers

The flowers are chosen for their bright appearance and also for their textural interest, as the arrangement will be viewed from a distance. Pink, red, green, orange, yellow and white materials in dyed and natural hues provide the bright summertime colour theme, but most bold, complementary colours are suitable.

Hydrangeas with their imposing flowerheads are suitable material for filling. They are available in a range of colours: blue, all-russet, pale green or creamy white. Russet and green hydrangea heads are used in our featured display, but you can use other colours if you prefer. Alternatively, you may be able to order bleached and dyed hydrangea heads from the

ATTACHING THE HANGING RIBBON

1 Pierce the centre of the 25cm (10in) foam ball with a kitchen skewer. Push two 40cm (16in) lengths of stub wire through the hole, allowing about 5cm (2in) of the wires to protrude from the bottom of the ball. Bend both wires back on themselves to form hooks and pull them up into the bottom of the foam ball to anchor them in position.

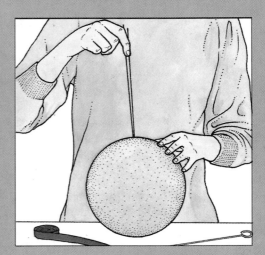

2 Using sharp wire cutters, trim the two pieces of wire that extend from the top of the ball to a length of 8cm (3in) and twist and bend them together to form a 'U'-shaped wire. Push the hooked wire over and press firmly down into the top of the foam ball so that no sharp ends are protruding from the surface of the ball. You are now ready to hang the ball.

3 Take a 1m (3ft) length of your chosen coloured ribbon and thread it through the wire loop. Make sure the ribbons are of even lengths on both sides of the loop and secure the ribbon to the wire loop by tying it firmly with a double knot. Tie both loose ends of ribbon together in an attractive bow with trailing ends or use a simple knot.

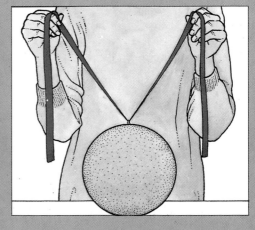

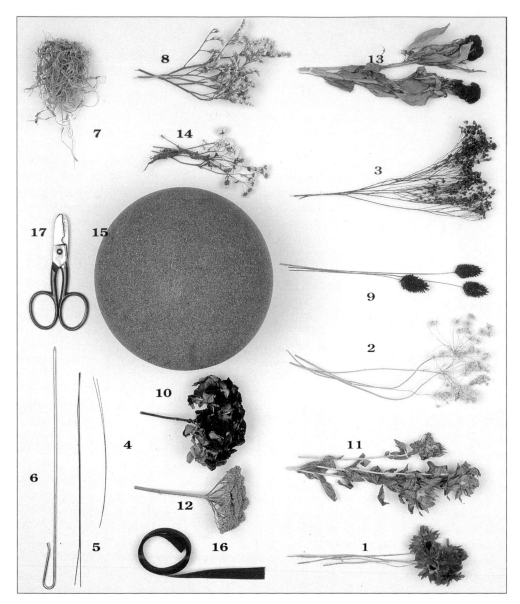

1 2 bunches of pink helipterum 2 1 bunch of white dill 3 1 bunch of green broom bloom 4 thin gauge stub wires 5 2 lengths of long, thick stub wire 6 skewer 7 1 bag of Spanish moss 8 2 bunches of statice 9 bunch of dyed pink phalaris 10 2 red and green hydrangea heads 11 1 bunch of green carthamus 12 1 bunch of yellow achillea 13 1 bunch of red cockscomb 14 1 bunch of white achillea 15 25cm (10in) dried flower foam ball 16 1m (3ft) red ribbon 17 scissors

seed pods could be substituted. For a blue scheme, use sea holly or wired-up echinops heads. If you wish to create a delicate look, try the delightful but extremely fragile seedheads of papermoon scabious.

Dill adds a light, lacy quality to the hanging ball. However, if you want an alternative, try dried ground elder, wild carrot or coriander heads.

DEEP COLOUR INTENSITY

Dark green dyed broom bloom adds depth and richness to the display. It will almost certainly have to be ordered from the florist. Suitable substitutes are bunched and wired dyed hair grass, yellow-green lady's mantle or, from the wild, densely packed sprigs of nipplewort.

Cockscomb has a natural, deep red colour and a velvet texture. There really isn't anything quite like it, but, as an alternative, use densely massed dried red roses, dahlias or craspedia heads to achieve a similar deep colour intensity to catch the eye.

Crimson dyed reed canary grass, or phalaris, adds contrasting texture and enhances the red colour theme of the cockscomb. You could use red dyed hare's-tail grass (*Lagurus ovatus*) instead, or tight bunches of red dyed quaking grass.

Dried Spanish moss (*Tillandsia usneoides*) is the most unusual ingredi-

florist in a range of 'designer' colours.

Like hydrangea, perennial statice, or sea lavender, is very familiar to arrangers as a staple filler for dried-flower displays. Here it is used as the initial cover for the grey foam ball to form a light background for the flowers. As an interesting substitute, you could use the slightly coarser annual statice or gypsophila.

COLOUR HIGHLIGHTS

Dense, flat heads of yellow achillea, or golden yarrow, contrast with the loose, rounded forms of other types of material. Also available are a paler yellow type and a delicate, pink-tinged form called 'Moonshine Pink'. The

closely related, but more delicate looking *Achillea ptarmica* 'The Pearl' also features; or large-flowered gypsophila, winged everlasting or miniature cluster-flowered everlasting could be used.

Helipterum, also called acroclinium or sunray, is a pink everlasting daisy with brittle stems that need careful handling. As well as the deep pink flowers used in this display, there are pale pink and white forms. Helichrysums, xeranthemums and rhodanthes are all available in pink and white; or use dried sweet william or wired hollyhock flowers instead.

Carthamus, or dyers' saffron, is readily available, but love-in-a-mist

MAKING
YOUR DRIED-FLOWER HANGING BALL

1 Attach the coloured ribbon to the foam ball (see box on page 19). Make 20 to 30 groups of four statice stems and trim these to 10cm (4in) long. Insert at intervals at an angle into the foam. Break two large hydrangea blooms into florets and trim to 5cm (2in) long. Wire with thin-gauge stub wire and insert adjacent to the statice.

2 Trim the stems of ten yellow achillea flowers to about 8cm (3in) long. Distribute them over the entire surface of the foam ball to introduce bright colour areas. Next, introduce the green carthamus. Cut the stems of 15 flowers to about 12cm (5in) long. Add them to the flower ball in groups of two or three.

3 Trim the side stems of pink helipterum flowers from the main stem and bind about eight or nine flowerheads together in bunches with thin-gauge stub wire. Make up about ten groups of flowers and insert them at random close to the foam to give the display a bright summery appearance.

4 Wire groups of five or six white achillea stems of varying lengths. To fill any remaining gaps between the flowerheads, bind together small handfuls of Spanish moss and attach them to the foam with stub wires bent into hairpin shapes or just 'float' the moss between the dried flowerheads to cover all the foam.

5 Suspend the ball above your work surface by the ribbon. Add the green broom bloom stems, cut to 5cm (2in) long, in groups of seven to eight stems. Remove the leaves from the red cockscomb. Trim the stems to 10cm (4in) long and place throughout the display to pick up the deep red of the ribbon.

6 Gently rotate the ball to see if there are any areas that require more colour. To build up brighter colour areas, add stems of deep pink phalaris. Cut the stems to about 10cm (4in) long and insert in groups of three or four at a time. Finally, add the dill in bunches of three or four stems cut to about 10cm (4in) long.

CHOOSING THE FOUNDATION

Here, a pre-formed, dried-flower florist's foam ball, 25cm (10in) in diameter, is used. To increase the size of the finished display, attach long stub wires to the dried material and don't press them right into the foam ball.

Try to avoid using fresh-flower foam balls, which might crumble when used dry. It is better to order a dried-flower foam ball from your florist.

CHOOSING THE SETTING

Height and space are important considerations when deciding where to hang your flower ball. The central stairwell in a spacious hall is ideal, since you can safely observe and enjoy the display from many levels as you use the stairs.

Hallways, especially in older houses, tend to have high ceilings which make them perfect for a pair or even a trio of hanging dried-flower balls. A single hanging ball in front of a fanlight above a door, where it could be seen from the outside as well as the inside, would look very effective.

Old houses often have central decorative roses on their living room ceilings, surrounding the lighting fixture. If your living room has low side-lighting and no central fixture, you could hang a dried-flower ball from the ceiling rose in a matter of a few minutes.

If you have limited space you could hang the flower ball from wall brackets above a piece of furniture, such as a sideboard or above a dining room table. Lastly, if the height allows, add a pretty ribbon bow to the bottom of the ball.

A simpler version of the hanging ball is made of hydrangea flower-heads, white and blue dyed statice, yarrow, golden cluster-flowered ever-lasting and yellow African daisies ent in this display. A relative of many epiphytic house plants (plants that live on the surface of another plant), Spanish moss isn't technically a moss at all, but its wiry stems and thread-like leaves give it a mossy appearance. As an alternative, you could use silvery grey reindeer moss instead.

DISPLAY CARE

If you hang your flower ball from a high ceiling, don't just forget about it and allow the flowers to fade and get dusty. Bring it down occasionally and replace any faded ingredients. Gently blow the dust and loose particles off the display with a hairdryer on a cool setting.

ALL SEWN UP

If you have a pretty sewing basket, use it as the container or inspiration for a delicate dried-flower arrangement. A sewing basket, with its small scale, soft lining and tiny but intricate tools calls for a pastel colour scheme. Our featured display uses soft pink with muted yellow, green, white, red and pale blue contrasts.

CHOOSING THE FLOWERS

Paeony is the most eye-catching flower used because it is larger than the others and is seen rarely in dried-flower displays. This popular herbaceous perennial garden flower is easy to grow and cheap to buy fresh, but it is difficult to preserve and therefore expensive to buy dried. It can be kiln-dried commercially or dried in a desiccant (see box on page 26). If you want to buy dried paeonies from a florist, order them well in advance.

A mop-head hydrangea flower, split into smaller clusters, is used as a filler, giving bulk to the display. Green florets tinged with maroon are shown but you could use pale green, creamy white, pink or blue for a softer look.

The dried red roses used are clearer in hue than the deep maroon dried roses more commonly available. Their fresh scarlet colour, with a hint of pink in the petals, keeps the display

Exchange your needles and thread for a collection of colourful dried flowers in this decorative, easy-to-make sewing-basket display

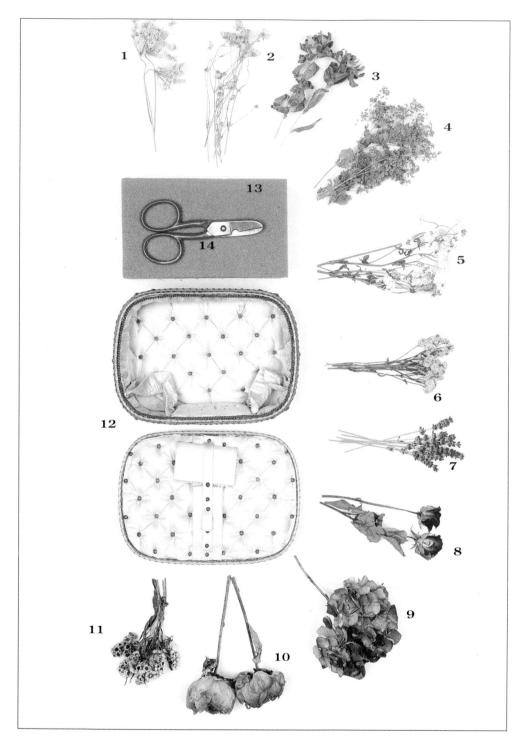

White achillea, *Achillea ptarmica* 'The Pearl', is like a larger version of gypsophila and makes a small scale filler for breaking up the solid outline of other flowers, such as hydrangeas and paeonies. Pale blue, dyed achillea is also used, but because its colour looks realistic and the dyed stems and leaves are hidden, it appears natural.

You may have to order the blue-dyed achillea in advance but natural white and blue-dyed gypsophila, especially the large, double-flowered types, could be substituted. If nothing else is available, use the small, lower sprigs and blue-tinged flower buds of blue and white larkspur. *Ammi majus* provides a lacy touch but small-flowered gypsophila or the dried green immature flowerheads of wild carrot could be substituted, or clusters of perennial white sea lavender, but choose a dainty variety as some have bulky blooms.

A LACY FILLER

Lady's mantle, also known as *Alchemilla mollis* is a hardy herbaceous perennial, easy to air-dry and fairly easy to buy. Another lacy filler if you are aiming to achieve a softer, greener effect, is dried cress, or lesser quaking grass.

Buttercups keep their fresh, spring-like yellow when dried, unlike other yellow flowers which often dry to a rich, autumnal gold or a papery beige. You could also use chamomile in its natural colour; tiny, wired flower buds

looking light and bright. You will probably have to order them in advance from your florist and they may be slightly more expensive than the dark red type.

ROSY HIGHLIGHTS

Dried peach, pink or creamy white roses could be substituted, or for a vibrant alternative, dried scarlet pompon dahlias. On a budget, scarlet helichrysums could be used instead, although you may have to buy several bunches of mixed helichrysum to get the number of scarlet flowers you need. You could also use a mixture of scarlet, pink and white helichrysum.

Pink-dyed strawflowers follow the rosy theme. Campion, globe amaranth, pale pink statice, helichrysum or the small, young buds of pink larkspur could be used instead.

MAKING
A BASKET DISPLAY

1 Cut the foam to fit the basket. Divide a hydrangea head into four florets with stems about 2.5cm (1in) long. Position one in the front left, one in the centre, one in the right front and one in the right back. Break off florets of lady's mantle. Place three or four on either side of the central hydrangea floret and a cluster around the front right floret.

2 Trim the carthamus stems to 8cm (3in) and place them behind the lady's mantle at the back of the basket, three stems to the left and three to the right. Push some foliage into the foam at different heights. Cut the white achillea stems to 8cm (3in) long. Bunch four groups of five to six stems around the edge of the basket to provide white highlights.

3 Fill out the display with pink strawflowers. Gather four groups of four flowerheads and place shorter groups towards the front and taller groups at the back. Add three large paeonies. Cut their stems down to about 12cm (5in). Position them slightly off centre to avoid rigid symmetry. Place two near the front and one to the centre left.

4 Untangle the buttercups stems and bunch them together in fairly large groups for colour impact. Add about three groups with 5cm (2in) stems. Work your way across the display from left to right. Position the small turquoise achillea flowers in groups next to the clusters of various pink flowers. Group together three or four stems about 8cm (3in) long.

5 Keep the foliage on the rose stems to add greenery to the arrangement. Group five stems together in the centre close to the green carthamus to create a bright, jewel-like effect and add fresh appeal. Balance this strong colour area with a second smaller group of two or three red roses inserted on the left side between the hydrangea and paeony.

6 Add a group of 12cm (5in) stems of lavender. Place 18 stems in the centre back. Allow them to stand upright to form a crown above the rest of the display. The display is now full and it is difficult to insert more flowers, so float the *Ammi majus* stems between the other flowers. Tuck stems in securely and they will be held in position by the clustered flowers.

PRESERVING PAEONIES

Single or semi-double paeony varieties are easier to dry than fully double types. Line a shoe box with waxed paper, then place a 1cm (½in) layer of warm silica gel (available from chemists) in the bottom of the box. Use dry flowers, cut just before their prime, placed right-way-up and spaced well apart in the box. Carefully sift warm, dry silica gel over the flowers, using a paintbrush to work the desiccant in between the petals. Continue until there is a 2.5cm (1in) layer of desiccant over the blooms. Cover the box and leave in a warm, dry place, such as an airing cupboard, for about a week. When all the petals feel papery and bone dry, they are ready for use in your dried-flower displays.

of bright yellow helichrysum or the ball-shaped yellow seed pods of common flax (*Linum usitatissimum*).

Carthamus, or safflower, is used in its immature stage, when it resembles prickly rosebuds about to open. If you can only get fully open blooms, either use them as they are or carefully snip off the bright orange thistle-like bracts with small scissors. You could also use large, green love-in-a-mist seed pods as an alternative.

Lavender provides spikiness, subtle colour and fragrance. You can buy it easily or air dry your own. Pick it just before it is at its prime, when half the tiny flowers are open. Always handle lavender by the stem; the older it is, the more fragile it becomes. Save any heads that fall off for adding to pot pourri or using in lavender bags.

CHOOSE THE CONTAINER

Sewing baskets can be made of several different types of material, but handwoven wicker or raffia ones are inexpensive and form a natural part-

nership with dried flowers. If you are a keen collector, there are many types of Victorian sewing baskets and boxes worth searching out. Among the most beautiful are velvet-covered sewing boxes with gilded metal strap-work, and papier mâché sewing boxes inlaid with shell or mother-of-pearl, often with realistic flowers painted on the black surface. There are also charming, less expensive, shell-covered boxes sold as souvenirs in Victorian sea-side resorts. Or you could use a particularly pretty, empty, chocolate box or an old jewellery box from a secondhand shop.

CHOOSING THE SETTING

If you are careful you could use this display to decorate a sewing table but it would probably be more convenient on a bedroom dressing table or vanity unit. If you want to place it on a windowsill, choose a lidded box and angle the lid to protect the flowers from direct sunlight.

People are now starting to collect old-fashioned, cast-iron sewing machine stands to use as occasional tables. If you are lucky enough to have one, place this arrangement on the top as the perfect finishing touch. Keep the display free from dust by gently sweeping particles away with a small, soft brush or a hair-dryer on a cool setting. Revitalise a worn display by mending broken stems and creating new stems for broken flower-heads (see box below).

If necessary, remove damaged plant material and rearrange the remaining material in a new display, add new material to the old, or discard battered material and reform the old display into several smaller ones. Bedraggled roses can be tidied by hand and broken flower petals can be attached with glue.

Faded displays have an old-world charm, but if you want your arrangement to retain its colour, remember to keep it away from strong light.

REPAIRING HOLLOW STEMS

Delicate dried flowers can be damaged easily but many stems can be repaired if they snap in half. To repair a break in a hollow-stemmed flower or seedhead such as carthamus, poppy, onion, dahlia, achillea or larkspur, insert a piece of stub wire at least 5cm (2in) long into the top piece of the stem, leaving at least 5cm (2in) of wire exposed.

Push the lower piece of the stem over the exposed length of stub wire until the two pieces of stem meet to form a neat invisible join, covering the wire completely. Stems can easily be extended in the same way. Slide a piece of stub wire into the stem and conceal it by wrapping gutta-percha tape around it. The flower can now be used on a long stem in a display.

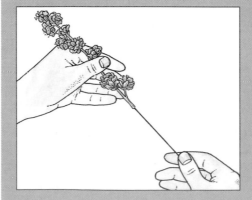

LUCKY HORSESHOE

This dried flower horseshoe is as pretty as a bridal bouquet and, unlike a fresh flower bouquet, will provide a permanent memento of the wedding day. As a traditional symbol of good luck, a horseshoe is a perfect going-away present.

A dried-flower horseshoe can be made well before the wedding day and stored; it simply needs to be kept in a dry place out of direct sunlight.

THE BASIC DESIGN

You don't need a ready-shaped base or frame for this design. The horseshoe is built up of dried flowers taped to a medium-gauge, straight stub wire, about 35cm (14in) long, although you could make it larger or smaller. The stub wire is bent into shape as you proceed, and the wired stems of the flowers provide strength and rigidity to the base.

The flowers, foliage and seed pods are used in bold clusters, and the sequence of groups is identical on both sides to create a symmetrical effect. To achieve an authentic horseshoe shape, the flowers, foliage and seed pods are built up more densely at the rounded bottom of the curve.

CHOOSING THE FLOWERS

The bride's choice of fresh flowers for the wedding can inspire the choice of dried flowers for the horseshoe. The flowers can match the wedding colour scheme or the going-away outfit, or can be based on the traditional bridal colours of white and pale cream.

The horseshoe featured contains bleached broom bloom, bleached and dyed hydrangea florets, love-in-a-mist seed pods, honesty seed cases, dried miniature roses and eucalyptus leaves.

Broom bloom has the delicacy of gypsophila, but the slender stems are tougher and easier to work with. Broom bloom is available in many

Give the bride a memorable send-off with this good luck token

colours, and usually has to be ordered in advance. You could use pale, pink-dyed broom bloom, or the fashionable pale peach instead.

Honesty is a biennial garden plant

WIRING A RIBBON BOW

Cut the ribbon to a length of 60cm (24in). Holding one end firmly in one hand and leaving a small tail, loop the ribbon into a figure of eight. The size of the loop determines the size of the finished bow. Holding the central point firmly, make a second figure of eight on top of the first. Continue building up the layers of ribbon loops. Bind a stub wire round the central point to secure the bow. Twist the wire together to form a stem for insertion into the display. Leave the ribbon tails long and trailing or cut short, as preferred.

1 1-2 stems of dried miniature roses **2** 1-2 stems of unbleached broom **3** 1-2 stems of unbleached honesty seed cases **4** 8-10 flat leaves **5** 15 love-in-a-mist seed pods **6** 12-15 dyed hydrangea petals **7** long length of ribbon **8** medium gauge stub wires **9** green gutta-percha tape **10** scissors

and, once it has seeded itself, it is established almost forever. Honesty's purple flowers appear in spring and are followed by bright green seed pods which turn to silver as they age. The honesty used in the horseshoe is dried ripe, thus retaining an attractive green tinge. If you are using honesty from your garden and want the silver effect, peel the papery covers off the seed pods to reveal the silver inner pod. Shop-bought honesty is usually ready peeled. Always handle honesty with great care; the seed pods can shatter easily and spoil the effect.

Bleached dyed hydrangea florets are available in several colours and look far more exotic than natural hydrangeas. You will probably have to order dyed florets in advance.

Dried miniature roses have a delicacy and charm, reminiscent of the small fairy and floribunda roses. You could use deep pink, red or creamy-white miniature roses instead, or single-blossomed, dried hybrid tea roses.

This horseshoe uses large, rounded leaves to add bulk and contrast to the display. Any similar, flat, dried leaves can be included. In particular, eucalyptus foliage would be an appropriate choice as it is sold fresh in a range of leaf shapes and sizes. Try to buy a

similar variety, and hang the branches upside down to dry for a week or so.

Love-in-a-mist seed pods look like tiny balloons, and are stocked by most outlets that sell dried flowers. As an alternative you could use wired clusters of hop or physocarpus seed pods.

GIVE THE FLOWERS A SHINE

Once you have made the lucky horseshoe, you can give it an attractive, protective coating of polyurethane varnish. Spray the horseshoe outdoors or place it on a piece of newspaper in a well-ventilated room to protect your

furnishings. Hold the spray can of varnish 30-40cm (12-16in) from the horseshoe and spray the plant materials evenly. Allow to dry, and apply a second coat, if necessary.

LOOKING AFTER THE DISPLAY

It may be tempting to display the dried-flower horseshoe on a wall but with exposure to sunlight and atmospheric moisture this means the display will probably only last about a year. Keeping the horseshoe in a tissue-filled cardboard box will ensure that it lasts much longer.

ASSEMBLING
YOUR LUCKY HORSESHOE

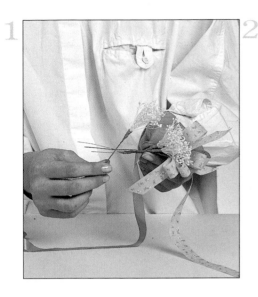

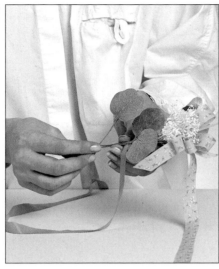

1 Make two wired ribbon bows (see box opposite). Leave a long length of ribbon trailing from one bow to form the handle. Wire four or five sprigs of broom into florets and cover the wire with gutta-percha tape. Place the bow with the ribbon tail and the florets at one end of a stub wire and stagger the florets.

2 Wire four flat leaves individually. Stitch fine stub wire through the central vein about two-thirds up the leaf. Pull the wire through and draw both ends together. Twist one wire around the remaining wire stem. Cover the wire with tape. Position the leaves so that they overlap each other and are lying just below the bleached broom florets.

3 Bind the artificial stems of the leaves to the stub wire with gutta-percha tape. Wire two or three small sprigs of miniature roses into florets. Cover any exposed wire with gutta-percha tape. Position the rose florets so they sit just below the flat leaves and secure the stems with gutta-percha tape. Ensure that the flowers are all facing in the same direction.

4 Group together six love-in-a-mist seed pods and place them underneath the miniature rose florets. Tape down the stems. Position five or six honesty seed cases just below the love-in-a-mist and tape them to the wire as before. Bend the wire gently as you proceed so it forms the curve of the horseshoe. Take care not to crush the flowers when doing this.

5 At the bottom of the curve stop grouping the flowers into florets and place them individually, making sure that you achieve an even distribution of all the materials. Wire the dyed hydrangea into florets of about three or four petals. Introduce these into the bottom of the curve. Repeat the same sequence of flowers in reverse order.

6 Before you put the last group of broom in position, make the ribbon handle. Tie the trailing end of ribbon to the second ribbon bow. Firmly attach the broom and the ribbon to the wire end with tape to complete the horseshoe shape. Make sure that the two sides match. Trim the ends of the ribbon and check that it is strong enough to hold the horseshoe.

KITCHEN
HIGHLIGHTS

It's easy to overlook the potential of a kitchen as a location for a flower display since it is so often busy and crowded. However, even in the smallest kitchen, there's usually space for a permanent arrangement of dried flowers. One obvious place for a display is the empty space on the top of your kitchen cupboards or dresser.

Purpose-built kitchen storage units can reach the ceiling, but most standard, manufactured storage units are installed leaving a small space above them. In the jargon of interior decora-tion, this gap is liable to be 'dead' space, because it is too high for easy access and too awkward for keeping items needed daily. Also, heat rises, making the space just under the ceiling hotter and stuffier than the rest of the room, and so it is not really suit-able for storing even tinned goods.

Such a dark, high-level space can look empty and this is where dried flowers come to the rescue for it is a bonus not a drawback to have a dried flower display tucked out of the way where it won't be disturbed.

SPECIAL CONSIDERATIONS

Most cut flowers in the home are dis-played at or below eye level: you look across at them, or slightly down onto them, in the same way that you do when you build up the arrangements. And, except in unusual circum-stances, you can get close to the flow-ers, even touch them if you want to. When building up high-level displays, such as this one, you have to take extra care that the flowers will be seen to their best advantage, as they will always be viewed from a distance. Obviously, you won't want to crane your neck all the time, looking at the flowers, so before beginning the arrangement, take a close look at your chosen spot from the place where you will look at it most often.

You will find that the farther away you are from the display, the easier it is to see. Up close, the angle of vision is steep, and the front of the storage unit, especially if it has a lip or cornice, may well conceal some of the flowers. If necessary, you can rest the display on a small base, such as a pile of newspapers, to build up its height. Unlike a standard front-facing arrangement, the upright flower stems of this cupboard-top display should be angled forward for increased visibilty, rather than inserted vertically.

WORKING TO SIZE

Generally, the closer the flowers are to the front of the units, the better. As an attractive variation, if the storage units do not have doors, allow some of the flowers to hang over the edge of the unit, either at the front or the sides. That way, the display becomes more of an integral part of the room. This is especially effective in a long, narrow, galley-type kitchen, where you can't stand far enough back from the flowers to see them properly. It's awkward working or even making final adjustments from a stepladder. Ideally, the display should fit exactly, so you can just slip it into place. Measure the area you are working to before you start (see the boxes on the right and on page 32 for details), and don't forget to allow for the thickness of the extra base, if you're using one.

Lastly, before you put the flowers in place, give the surface a thorough dust, or wipe down with a damp rag and allow it to dry thoroughly.

CHOOSING THE FLOWERS

If you have dried-flower displays elsewhere in your kitchen or dining room, such as in the middle of the table or on a windowsill, repeat the colours and choice of flowers in your high-level display for a unified theme. If you are starting from scratch, the colour scheme of the room can give you a sound basis from which to work and if your best set of china is on display, you can pick up the main colours in that and repeat them in the arrangement.

The space above the storage units is often dark, so light flowers in pastel colours, pinks, yellows and whites will show up best. Dark wine reds, deep browns and blues would recede into the background and just add to the gloom, although a few touches of deep colour can add interest to a bright display. Light bright colours show up better from a distance, too, another important consideration when designing a high-level display.

The colour scheme of this display is based on pinks, yellows and white. A mixture of inexpensive dried flowers is used: pink helichrysums, pink helipterums, pink-dyed broom bloom, pink-dyed carthamus, yellow achillea, white achillea, white sea lavender, pinky mauve hydrangea florets, and, lastly yellowy-green lady's mantle (*Alchemilla mollis*).

Helichrysum, helipterum, sea lavender, yarrow and hydrangea are commonly used flowers, not particularly rare or exotic but attractive and easily available from most dried-flower stockists. Others such as carthamus and achillea are more unusual, and may well have to be ordered in advance.

Helichrysum, also known as straw-flower, comes in a range of colours as

A display of dried flowers transforms a potentially 'dead' space on the top of kitchen cupboards into an exciting focal point. This beautiful arrangement provides a melody of pinks, yellows and natural whites

SIZING-UP THE ARRANGEMENT

1 This style of arrangement is designed to fit in a specific space between the top of a cupboard or dresser and the ceiling. Measure the dimensions carefully before you begin. You will need to know the exact height to which you are working and the maximum width of each display – particularly if you want to put two arrangements on top of one cupboard.

2 The height and width of the display are determined as you start arranging, when you are building up the basic fan shape. Cut the stems of your first few flowers to establish the maximum height and width of the display. Remember to leave a small gap around the display to give it enough visual breathing space. A small space between the tops of the flowers and the ceiling is most important.

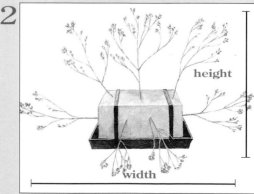

well as the strong pink used in this display, so replace with creamy white or paler pink blooms if you feel the concentration of dark pink is too over-whelming. The daisy-like helipterum flowers are also available in a wide variety of natural and dyed colours.

UNUSUAL FLOWERS

White achillea, or sneezewort (*Achillea ptarmica*), and yellow achil-lea, or yarrow (*A. filpendulina*), are closely related but quite different in appearance. Yarrow has large, flat, round 'plates' of densely-packed golden florets, traditionally popular for autumnal dried-flower displays. White achillea is composed of tiny clusters of small, round, double flow-ers, almost like outsized gypsophila. The variety 'The Pearl' is a popular hardy garden perennial, and is so

DESIGNING TO FIT

Place the finished display in position on top of the cupboard as near to the front as possible. If there is a deep lip or cornice on the cupboard and the arrange-ment is not clearly visible from below, then lift it up by putting it on top of a pile of newspapers or magazines. Check that the display looks full enough and fill in any remaining spaces with extra flowers.

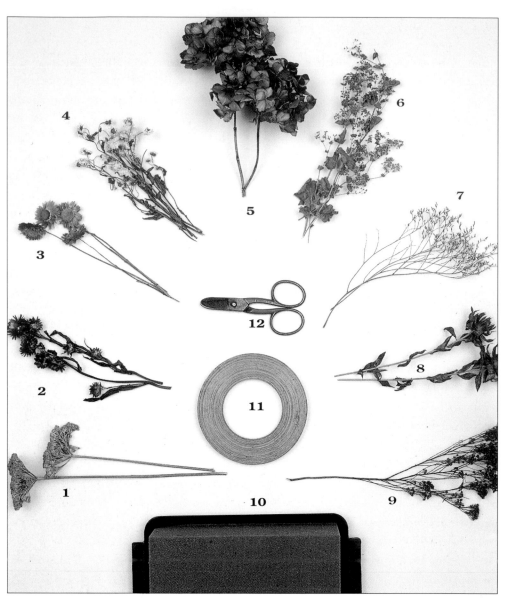

1 2 bunches of yellow achillea **2** 1 bunch of helipterum **3** 1 bunch of pink helichrysum **4** 2 bunches of white achillea **5** 5 hydrangea heads **6** 1 bunch of lady's mantle **7** 1 bunch of sea lavender **8** 1 bunch of dyed carthamus foliage **9** 1 bunch of dyed broom bloom **10** 23cm (9in) block of dry florist's foam **11** adhesive tape **12** scissors

tough and easy to grow that it can be invasive. All achilleas air dry easily; just strip the leaves and hang them upside down in a dry, well-ventilated spot. At a pinch, you could use pearl everlasting (*Anaphalis spp*), or a dou-ble variety of dried white gypsophila as a substitute for the white achillea.

Pink-dyed broom bloom and pink-dyed carthamus are also 'specialist' flowers, though larger garden centres or the home furnishing sections of major department stores may stock them. Dyed broom bloom is bleached

before being dyed, so it loses all trace of its natural colour. It comes dyed in a wide range of different shades.

THE CONTAINER

Unlike most cut flower displays, in this one the container should not be prominently displayed. It is more important to get a full view of the flow-ers. A flat, plastic rectangular florist's tray, 23cm (9in) long is ideal. These are inexpensive and come in a range of sizes and shapes, to fit the sizes and shapes of florist's foam blocks.

A COLOURFUL
CUPBOARD-TOP DISPLAY IN SIX STEPS

1 Tape the dry foam to the tray with adhesive tape. Cut the lavender stems to 23cm (9in). Make a fan with eight to ten sprigs to set the width and height of the display. In a front-facing display the back should be straight and the sides pieces should be inserted at right angles. As this display is to be viewed from below, the back and the sides should be angled forwards.

2 Cut the white achillea slightly shorter than the sea lavender. Make little bunches of five or six stems and insert them into the foam, following the lines of the sea lavender. Gather together little bunches of six to eight stems of lady's mantle. Make about ten bunches. Insert them in the arrangement, filling in between the sea lavender and achillea.

3 Wire some short stems of hydrangea heads. Holding them very firmly, feed the medium gauge stub wire through the tiny stems under the flowerhead. Wrap one side of the wire round the other to form a false stem to insert into the foam. Wire four or five flowerheads in the same way and insert them evenly throughout the arrangement to provide strong colour.

4 Tip the arrangement backwards and insert the yellow achillea along what will be the front of the display. By tipping the arrangement backwards you can build up plenty of flowers at the front. Insert the stems at an angle so that the flowers hang over the edge of the cupboard. Insert two or three more achillea stems evenly all round the display.

5 Gather little bunches of dyed acrolinium flowers in your hand so that the stems are all of equal length. Sometimes the stems are brittle so you need to wire them together to insert them into the foam. Otherwise, hold the stems at the bottom so they don't snap when inserted. Place ten bunches evenly throughout the display. Do the same with the pink helichrysum.

6 Insert 10-12 stems of the dyed carthamus evenly throughout the display. Finish by adding as many stems of dyed broom bloom as is necessary to fill in any holes. Take the finished arrangement to its final location. Check that the flowers look full enough from underneath and the display fits comfortably in the available space. Fill in any gaps with open flowers.

BEDSIDE POSY

For a lasting memento of Mothering Sunday, try making this inexpensive, dried-flower posy. As you will probably have to buy a bunch of each of the flowers used, you should have more than enough material to make two posies. Create one for yourself and another as a gift, or make a pair to give, as an extra special gesture of appreciation.

This display is a variation on the traditional posy theme. Posies are designed to be held in the hand, and are often built up in concentric circles of flowers, round a single, central bud or open blossom. Fashionable Victorian ladies carried special posy holders, often collapsible, in which posies could be rested when the owner tired of holding them. This arrangement, with its little lace collar and mounded flowers, captures all the charm of traditional posies, and the attractive glass container is both an integral part of the display and provides built-in support.

A delicate dried-flower posy with a pretty lace collar is an ideal gift for Mothering Sunday

CHOOSING THE FLOWERS

The colour theme for this posy is pink and white, a traditionally feminine choice. It is therefore the natural choice for Mothering Sunday, an occasion that celebrates the role of motherhood.

Helichrysum, or strawflowers, are becoming increasingly available in single colour bunches. If possible, choose a creamy white bunch with flowers in all stages of development: fully open, half open and in bud. Try to avoid bunches with over-blown flowers — those with a fluffy central disc, and petals that curve back from the centre. These flowers are liable to disintegrate at the slightest touch. If you can only get a mixed colour bunch, choose the one with the highest proportion of cream and pink flowers. Provided there are six usable blossoms, you will be able to get by with one bunch; otherwise, buy two bunches and save the darker-toned flowers for another arrangement.

Dried cream gypsophila adds a light, airy touch, continuing the delicate lacy theme through the display. You could use dried white gypsophila or dyed pale pink gypsophila as an alternative to the cream blooms. If you choose the pink, then it might be a good idea to use white statice or perhaps chamomile to keep an attractive balance of colours.

CHOOSING ROSEBUDS

The dried pink rosebuds are the most expensive ingredient in this display, but remember that one bunch supplies enough material to make two posies. On a tight budget, you could use the cheaper green carthamus buds, which are very similar in shape, instead. If you do, make sure you snip off any visible bright orange, central thistle heads as their colour will clash with the other flowers and spoil the overall effect of the posy.

Statice is sold in single-colour bunches, but a well-chosen mixed bunch of statice should contain a couple of stems with pink flowers, which is all you need. Again, any dark stems can be stored ready for use in other arrangements. White statice can also be used, especially if you have substituted pink flowers for some or all of the white ones illustrated.

USING DYED MATERIAL

Two ingredients in this display – chamomile and dock – are dyed pink. The overall effect is still natural looking because the dyed flowers vary in shade and tint – the dock just borders on orange and the chamomile is a pale, milky pink. When used in arrangements, pink-dyed flowers always create a more natural effect than bright blue, pure red or purple blooms, especially when displayed in large quantities. You may have to order the dyed flowers specially, although larger retail outlets often have a good selection of both natural coloured and dyed material.

Chamomile is yet another useful member of the daisy, or *Compositae*, family. Tea made from chamomile is both soothing and sleep inducing. Its flowerheads look like little velvet buttons standing on poker-straight stems and it is especially useful to fill in spaces in dried-flower arrangements. Like statice, chamomile comes in a range of artificial colours; dyed-pink chamomile is used here, but bleached white blooms would do equally well.

ADDING TEXTURE WITH SEEDHEADS

Pink-dyed dock seedheads are the most unusual ingredient in this dis-

WIRING A LACE COLLAR

Traditional posy shapes and lace seem to go together quite naturally since both have an old-fashioned feeling and epitomise Victorian elegance. To save yourself time you can buy ready-made and stiffened florist's lace circles in various sizes to fit onto posies, but for an extra-frilly effect, try making a 'composite' collar, as shown.

1 To decorate a 10cm (4in) diameter bowl, cut eight to ten pieces of lace 5cm (2in) in length. Pleat each piece of lace at the base and wrap the top 5cm (2in) of a 20cm (8in) stub wire round the base to hold the pleating in place.

2 Twist the remainder of the wire down to form an artificial stem. Insert the lace florets at an angle into the dry foam block to create a collar effect.

1 1 bunch of cream helichrysum **2** dyed pink dock **3** 1 bunch of love-in-a-mist seedheads
4 1 bunch of pink statice **5** 1 bunch of pink rosebuds **6** common chamomile (dyed pink)
7 1 bunch of cream gypsophila **8** pink lace **9** small pink glass bowl **10** dry foam **11** pink
ribbon **12** stub wire **13** scissors, and transparent glue

scatter them in your garden on a patch of bare earth. Rake the seeds in gently, and before long you should have your own love-in-a-mist garden.

CHOOSING THE CONTAINER

An inexpensive, three-legged, glass bowl, about 10cm (4in) across, is used for this arrangement. The pale pink tint of the glass adds emphasis to the feminine theme, but is not essential.

You could use an opaque white glass or china bowl instead. Either an antique Victorian milk glass or a good quality reproduction bowl would add equally well to the old-fashioned charm of this display. For this arrangement, it is best to avoid using a heavily patterned container which would detract from the intricate texture of the flowers themselves.

SELECTING THE DECORATIONS

Pale pink lace, 7.5cm (3in) wide, and deep pink ribbon, 2.5cm (1in) wide, add a festive and very feminine touch to this arrangement. Both of these materials should be available from a florist's shop, although you might have to make do with white lace, rather than pale pink. Florist's polyester lace and ribbon are used here because they are stiff, but you could also use ribbon or lace purchased from the haberdashery department of a fabric shop instead. Buy 1m (3ft 3in) of each – they are so inexpensive that it is worth having that little bit extra to ensure you have enough.

play. Its seed pods look a little like the dainty pink flowers of waxy bedding begonias. Dock is a pernicious weed, but in this arrangement it is put to good artistic use and provides the bulk of material for the posy.

Love-in-a-mist seedheads, like poppy seedheads, cannot possibly be confused with any other material.

They look like inflated green balloons, sometimes with maroon stripes, and occasionally with dried, bright blue petals still attached. Love-in-a-mist is a hardy annual, which is easy to cultivate and, once established in a garden, tends to self-seed. If any of the tiny black seeds fall out of the pods as you arrange the display, collect them and

CHOOSING THE SETTING

A small display such as this needs to be placed where it will not be dwarfed visually, and where its intricate beauty can be fully appreciated. A bedside table provides the ideal situation, but a dressing table or small writing desk would do equally well, provided the surrounding area is not too cluttered.

CREATING
A BEDSIDE POSY

1 Cut a foam block to fit the container and extend 2.5cm (1in) above the rim. If clear glass is used, line the container with lace to help hide the foam block. Glue the block to the base of the container, and allow to dry. Wire six to eight sections of lace (see box on page 35) and insert the wires into the side of the block; with the lace overlapping, to form a collar.

2 Cut 12 to 15 small sprigs, 5-7.5cm (2-3in) long, from the dock stem. Remove the lowest seed pods. Position the sprigs all over the foam to build up the basic posy shape, but do not hide the lace. Turn the container round as you proceed to check that the globe shape is building up symmetrically and that the sprigs of dock are distributed evenly.

3 Cut 18 to 20 love-in-a-mist stems, 5-7.5cm (2-3in) long, and insert one seed pod upright in the centre to establish the height of the display and insert the remaining seed pods radiating outwards from the central pod. Again, place the shorter stems towards the edge. Break off small sprigs of statice, 5-7.5cm (5-3in) long, and use them to continue filling in the display.

4 Begin adding the larger flowerheads to the display. Cut the stems of six to eight cream helichrysum, about 5-7.5cm (2-3in) long as before. Helichrysum stems are fragile so handle them very carefully. Insert in a loose circle above the rim. Any flowerheads that break off can be wired up and inserted or put aside for use later in another arrangement or pot pourri display.

5 Cut five to six rosebuds stems, 5-7.5cm (2-3in) long. Remove and save any leaves for use another time. Holding them by their stems, insert the rosebuds randomly, filling any gaps where the foam block is visible. Add small bunches of gypsophila and chamomile, in groups of three or four sprigs of a single type for strength and to give maximum visual impact.

6 To add lustre to the display, make six to eight ribbon florets. Cut the ribbon into lengths 8cm (3in) long. Fold each length into three pleats, then bind light-gauge stub wire tightly around the base of the ribbon to secure it. Insert the wired florets into the posy to fill out any bare spots. Inspect the display, turning it slowly round and making any necessary adjustments.

SWAGS
& SPICES

Wall space is perfect for displaying dried flowers, especially in a small house where horizontal space is limited or where babies and small children make table displays impractical. This swag brightens up kitchen shelves and would be an ideal gift for a friend keen on cookery. It combines dried flowers, cereal grains, herbs, spices and dried mushrooms, on plaited raffia.

Raffia is made of fibre from the raffia palm and is used for making baskets, string and mats. Before the days of plastic, raffia was indispensable in the garden, for tying up and training plants. Some garden centres still sell raffia skeins. Craft shops often sell it, but few florists stock it so ask your florist to order it from a wholesaler.

You can make a simple raffia swag by tightly tying a long skein of raffia crossways every 10-15cm (4-6in), then inserting decorative dried material at each tie. Plaiting takes slightly longer, but gives a more finished and professional look. Decide how long you want your swag to be, then attach one end of the skein to a strong vertical support such as a chair or a coat hook. Divide the raffia strands into three equal sections, then weave the right and left sections towards the middle, in turn, just as if you were plaiting hair. Pull the raffia tight to give a dense finish. Cut the plait at the required length, tie tightly with a piece of raffia 5-7.5cm (2-3in) from the bottom to create a tail, then trim the ends evenly.

CHOOSING THE FLORAL MATERIALS

No dyed materials are used here, in keeping with the natural food theme, but the swag's natural colours have a warm glow. Deep pink helichrysum goes very well with a wide range of colours, but cream helichrysum would suit a neutral colour scheme in pine or an off white kitchen. In a French provincial-style kitchen try cheerful yellow or deep red helichrysum flowers for a lively touch.

Blue larkspur, an annual form of delphinium, contrasts effectively with pink, in form as well as in colour. Larkspur is available in pale and deep shades of pink and blue and in white, so you could repeat the pink of the helichrysum with larkspur, or combine white larkspur with cream-coloured helichrysum. When cutting larkspur flower spikes for the swag, save the immature flower spikes lower down the main stem; the tight green buds look very good in miniature arrangements.

Clusters of wheat are used here to contrast with the flowers and to add culinary overtones. Any similar grain spikes could be used, perhaps riper, golden ears rather than the slightly green-tinged ones here.

The flax seedheads here look like

This cheerful array of cereals, dried flowers, spices and mushrooms adds a splash of colour to a country-style kitchen

little golden baubles on wiry stems. Common flax (*Linum usitatissimum*) is a hardy blue flowered annual. You could use clusters of wild nipplewort (*Lapsana communis*) seed pods, mimosa or tansy flowers instead.

CHOOSING THE HERBS & SPICES

Fresh garlic is the largest of the herbs and spices used in this swag, and is widely available. Thought to have originated in Asia, it has been cultivated near the Mediterranean since the days of the ancient Egyptians and is now grown in warm countries all over the world. Look for plump, fresh, unblemished bulbs, with all the cloves intact and no trace of grey mould. Press the bulbs slightly; they should feel hard, and be heavy for their size. Choose ones with long stalks for ease in wiring.

Cinnamon sticks add their warm colour and spicy smell to the swag. They are the rolled inner bark of the tropical cinnamon tree, a small evergreen related to bay and laurel. The cinnamon tree is a native of Sir Lanka and was unknown to the rest of the world until the Dutch arrived there in the seventeenth century.

Whole nutmegs make another unusual decorative addition to the swag. Nutmeg is the seed of an evergreen tropical tree, *Myristica fragrans*. Although commonly sold ground and powdered, few spices have the delicious pungency of freshly grated nutmeg. You could substitute our fea-

WIRING MUSHROOMS & GARLIC

Make a short, right-angled leg at one end of a piece of stub wire. It should be a little shorter than the length of the mushroom or garlic stem. Push it against the stem, then bend the long leg back over it, and tightly encircle both the stem and the short leg of wire several times.

With mushroom stems which flare at the bottom, tightly wrap the end of the wire around the middle several times rather than making a wire leg.

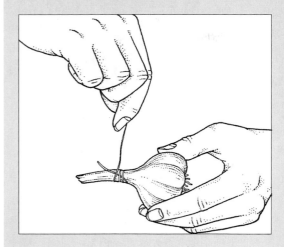

tured spices with chestnuts, walnuts, brazil nuts, hazelnuts or pecans.

Dried chillis would add an exotic touch and rich colour to the swag, but take care and wear gloves when handling them, since they can cause rashes. Dried bay leaves would also make an attractive addition, and are widely available although quite brittle. Using fresh bay leaves from the garden is an easier and more practical alternative; just wire them onto the swag and let them dry in position.

Dried mushrooms are expensive, and are available from gourmet food shops, particularly Italian. You can order them from your florist, but ask for stemmed mushrooms, rather than bracket fungi. It is a much better idea to collect wild mushrooms yourself in the autumn and dry them at home, over a night storage heater or radiator, or in a warm airing cupboard.

MAKING THE SWAG
All the floral material and most of the edible ingredients in this arrangement are wired to the raffia plait. Because of the plait's thickness and density, it is difficult to push the wire through. Here, thick, heavy-gauge

stub wire is used to wire the bunches of wheat, helichrysum and larkspur to the plait. Push the wire through the less dense areas of the swag, where two strands of plaited raffia cross. Adjust and position the dried material once it has been wired on.

Match the strength of the wire to the strength of the stems, as well as to its purpose. Thin, light gauge stub wire is used for the lighter, delicately stemmed flax although it is harder to get it through the plait. For wiring the garlic and dried mushrooms, medium gauge wire offers the required strength and flexibility. If you don't already have several gauges of stub wire and have to buy wire just for this display, choose just the medium gauge.

Quick-drying glue, as used here, is the easiest way to attach the cinnamon sticks and nutmeg. Alternatively, you could drill holes and thread wire through the nutmegs, and also wire the cinnamon sticks.

CHOOSING THE SETTING
A kitchen is the most obvious place to hang this garlic-studded swag, but a country-style dining room would be equally suitable. The swag will stay in better condition in a dining room, out of the kitchen, away from the oven and cooking steam. Dried flowers shed particles so avoid placing the swag where debris can fall into food.

Ensure the display is well-lit: place it perhaps between two kitchen or dining-room windows, or as a pair on either side of a window, or use it to brighten up the blank end of a kitchen cupboard.

Without the garlic, the swag loses its kitchen feeling and, with the addition of more flowers, could decorate a living room or hall.

CARING FOR YOUR SWAG
Garlic cloves eventually shrivel and go mouldy, depending on how fresh they were when they were bought. Carefully remove the old garlic bulbs, without disturbing adjacent flowers and spices, and replace them with fresh ones. Don't be tempted to cook with the old garlic as it would give food a rancid flavour.

1 1 skein of raffia, plaited, and trimmed to 80cm (32in) **2** 25 ears of wheat **3** 20 stems of pink helichrysum **4** 6 cinnamon sticks **5** 6 whole nutmegs **6** 3-4 dried stemmed mushrooms **7** 2 or 3 heads of garlic **8** 25 stems of flax seedheads **9** 25 stems of blue larkspur **10** light, medium and heavy-gauge stub wire **11** floristry scissors, and strong transparent glue

CREATING
A KITCHEN HANGING SPICE PLAIT

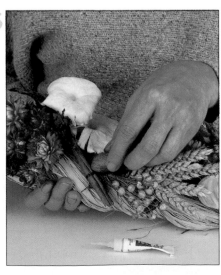

1 Wire clusters of four or five ears of wheat into six bunches, using heavy-gauge wire. Leave a long wire stem. Push the wire stems through to the back of the raffia plait so that the wheat bunches face upwards and are on a diagonal slant. Make a loop where the wire emerges and push the free leg of wire sideways through the raffia to secure it firmly.

2 Cut the top 10cm (4in) off the larkspur spikes. Make five bunches of five spikes each. Attach them diagonally to the swag, at a different angle to the wheat. Use the larkspur to overlap the base of the wheat stems, and conceal the wiring. At the tail, attach one larkspur bunch facing downwards, again overlapping the wheat but angled away from it.

3 Using thin stub wire, wire five bunches of flax seedheads with five stems each. Cut the stems about 10cm (4in) long. Place the flax bunches at the base of the larkspur to conceal the wires. Manipulate the thin stub wire to get it through the raffia. Arrange each cluster so that the different bunches are angled away from each other to create a spray-like effect.

4 Make four bunches of dark pink helichrysum. Use five flowers for each bunch, including buds as well as fully open flowers. Carefully wire the bunches to the swag, directly below the flax, concealing the wiring. Angle the helichrysum bunches in a different direction to the flax. Their flowerheads create an attractive mound at the base of each cluster.

5 Adjust the flowers and wheat then add the herbs and spices. Wire the mushrooms and garlic bulbs (see box on page 39). Use the flat, umbrella-shaped mushrooms to cover large areas of raffia and any messy wires. Use the garlic bulbs to fill any gaping spaces on the sides of the display; two were used here but use more or less as you require.

6 Glue pairs of cinnamon sticks and nutmegs onto the plait. Follow the glue manufacturer's instructions and allow the correct drying time. Finally, carefully turn the plait over and with strong scissors or wire-cutters remove any long wires that might scratch the wall or kitchen fittings. Attach a wire loop to the top of the swag to hang it on the wall.

MODERN
MOSS PYRAMID

In a modern, geometric display, such as the featured pyramid, flowers and seedheads play a minor role due to their neutral shades. Rather, it is the flat planes, straight lines and sharp angles of the pyramid that are the distinguishing features. Making an arrangement with a limited number of materials in a rigid form can prove an exciting challenge. The principle of using straight lines and highlighting sharp angles also can be applied to other geometric shapes, such as obelisks, squares or rectangles. Cover the foam shape with a carpet of textured moss or similar material and emphasize the outlines with rows of flowers.

TOPIARY IDEAS

This pyramidal arrangement with its sculptured shape is inspired by the ancient art of topiary – the training and pruning of trees and shrubs into decorative forms – which dates from Roman times. Most people are familiar with the clipped round bay trees on their short straight stems, but in ancient Roman days, pruning and training evergreens such as box, elaeagnus, yew, holly and rosemary into fantastic shapes was a far more popular activity than it is today. Centuries later, the Renaissance saw a renewed interest in topiary, and many famous Italian Renaissance gardens sported examples on a grand scale. As well as clipping evergreens into the simple traditional topiary shapes such as the pyramid, globe

and cube, they were often placed one on top of the other, with stretches of bare trunk in between. There were also bizarre and exotic shapes, such as vases and urns, arches and temples, men, women and apes, and even popes and cardinals. The craze for topiary gardens spread first to France and Holland and reached England in the seventeenth century.

Modified versions of all simple geometric forms can be made with florist's foam blocks and dried reindeer moss. One, two or three shapes can be covered with dried moss and displayed on a dowel or natural branch 'trunk'.

CHOOSING THE FOUNDATION

A large block of dried foam, 30 x 60cm (12 x 24in) is used in the pyramid featured here; the dimensions of the finished foundation are roughly 30cm (12in) in height with a 30 x 30cm (12 x 12in) base. These large foam blocks are not normally stocked by florists and have to be ordered in advance from wholesalers. For details on making the foam pyramid, see the box on page 44.

CHOOSING THE MATERIAL

Making specific sculptured shapes requires plant material that can be compacted and built up gradually. Moss is ideal as it can be used to create a covering 'carpet' of plant material. Examples of tiny-headed, cluster-type flowers that can be used instead of moss include gypsophila, glixia,

Impressively elegant but restrained, this pyramid-shaped display makes a striking feature for an ultramodern room

statice and solidaster. They will all create a thick carpet-like effect, but it will not be as compact as moss.

Five bags of dried reindeer moss in its natural, silvery white colour are used for the pyramid. Reindeer moss is also available in a range of dyed colours including pale pink, fuchsia, creamy yellow, mauve, blue-grey, dark grey, spring green, deep green and russet. As reindeer moss usually has to be ordered in advance, check with your florist which other colours are available. Dyed reindeer moss can be expensive, however, and you may have to buy a whole box. It does not matter if you don't use it all in one display as reindeer moss will keep indefinitely if stored in a dry, airy place.

DECORATING WITH FLOWERS

The flowerhead and seed pod decorations play a very small role, like piped icing round the edge of a cake, but like icing, they provide an important finishing touch.

Echinops, or globe thistles, are unmistakable, and their round spiky seed pods fit in perfectly with the formal, geometric theme. There are no other flowers that resemble echinops closely, but silvery sea holly seedheads or silvery white poppy seedheads could be used instead.

Nigella, or love-in-a-mist, seed-heads are also hard to replace, They are cheap and widely available but, if necessary, any of the suggested substitutes for echinops would also be suitable.

Clusters of dried, blue-dyed botoa flowerheads are also used. Within a single bunch there is a subtle variation in colour, some being more silver or blue than others, but the general tone is similar to the reindeer moss. Dried, dyed chamomile could be used instead or, for a tiny, dot-like effect, clusters of glixia or stirlingia in various dyed colours. Flax seed pods, which resemble small baubles, are available, dyed blue grey, and these also could be substituted.

Choosing the setting

A house or flat with an ultramodern decor is most suitable for this style of display, offering a setting that is stark and uncluttered. In a house which is decorated in an old-fashioned 'cottagey' style, a globe-shaped moss display on a small 'trunk' might look more appropriate.

Alternatively, by inserting a trunk base into a smaller pyramid shape, the pyramid display can be transformed into a 'topiary' tree, which, again, would be more in keeping with a traditional setting. In both cases, sink the base of the trunk in plaster of Paris in a glazed or a terracotta pot, sprayed to match the colour of the reindeer moss.

SHAPING THE FOAM BLOCK

1 Stand the foam block upright on the work surface. Mark out a small 5 x 5cm (2 x 2in) square in the top centre of your block. This forms the top point of the pyramid. Using a sharp knife, keep slicing off the four edges in turn until you have pared down the block into four even planes 30cm (12in) deep.

2 Continue shaving away the foam until you have formed a flat-sided pyramid. At this stage, cut the block in half horizontally. The base of the pyramid should be 30cm (12in) wide and it should stand at a height of 30cm (12in). The moss and the flowerheads will disguise any irregularities in shape.

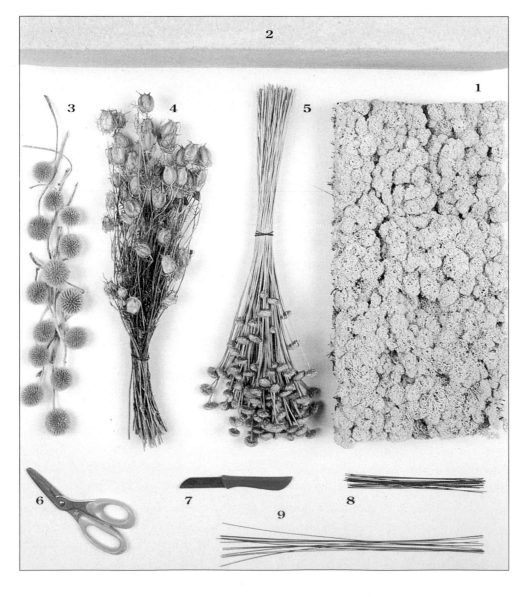

1 5 bags of reindeer moss 2 block of dry florist's foam 30 x 60cm (12 x 24in) 3 4 bunches of natural green echinops 4 4 bunches of love-in-a-mist seedheads 5 4 bunches of dyed botoa 6 scissors 7 florist's knife 8 10cm (4in) stub wires 9 25cm (10in) stub wires

MAKING
A GEOMETRIC PYRAMID DISPLAY

1 Cut the foam block into a pyramid shape (see box). Cut the bunch of 25cm (10in) stub wires into 5cm (2in) lengths and bend them into U-shaped pins. Soak the reindeer moss in water until soft and supple and place it on a kitchen towel to absorb the excess moisture. Break up the moss into small clumps and pin along the main lines of the pyramid to act as guidelines.

2 Start to fill in the sides of the pyramid with more clumps of reindeer moss. Pin the pieces of moss very close to each other so that there are no sections of exposed foam. The thick carpet of reindeer moss forms a neutral base for the decorations that follow. Continue until the entire foam base is covered with an even layer of textured moss on every side.

3 Add the echinops heads. Trim each stem to 5cm (2in). They are strong enough not to need wiring. Insert each echinops stem at regular 2.5cm (1in) intervals through the moss and into the foam in a row around the base of the pyramid. You will need at least 80 echinops heads to go round the whole of the foam base.

4 Wire the small mint-coloured botoa flowerheads into about 24 individual florets. For each bunch, group together four or five flowerheads and trim the stems to a length of 5cm (2in). Tightly bind the botoa stems with a 10cm (4in) length of stub wire and trim the wire to a length of 5cm (2in). This will create a false stem to insert the botoa stems into the foam.

5 Arrange the wired botoa bunches at even intervals along the edges of the pyramid to pick out the angles and create a strong geometrical effect. Insert six bunches from top to bottom along each of the four vertical lines of the pyramid. The dyed botoa bunches should be about 5-7cm (2-3in) apart. These flowerheads will add sharper definition to the pyramid shape.

6 To further define the shape and add textural interest, insert single love-in-a-mist seed pods. You will need about 40 seedheads. Insert them in every space in between the echinops heads, around the base of the pyramid and between the bunches of botoa along the four edges. Finish with a single seedhead placed in the top centre of the pyramid to define the apex.

A TROUBLE-FREE
BONSAI

True bonsai are outdoor trees, conifers or shrubs which are grown from seed in miniature containers and trained to resemble gnarled old specimens. They take many years to reach maturity and require a complex routine of feeding, watering, wiring, branch and root pruning, pinching out and repotting to keep them in good condition and to maintain the traditional shape. As a result, mature bonsai trees are expensive to buy and require a great deal of care and attention.

INSTANT SOLUTION

If you enjoy the look of a mature bonsai, but do not relish the expense or on-going commitment, this is the ideal solution: a convincingly lifelike bonsai

This lifelike tree is made from a forked branch topped with dyed green reindeer moss. Dried bun moss, achillea, pebbles and gravel form the landscape in the Japanese bonsai pan made of dried moss and a gnarled tree branch. It remains in perfect form indefinitely, needs only occasional dusting and is cheap and easy to make. The construction is quite straightforward: dried florist's foam in a bonsai pan forms the foundation; a forked branch represents the trunk of a tree; and dried moss is glued to small foam blocks to make the foliage. Lastly, a miniature landscape is created at the base of the tree with moss, pebbles, gravel and flowers.

TRADITIONAL BONSAI

Bonsai means 'plant in a tray'. The practice of dwarfing trees in a container and displaying them for contemplation and artistic appreciation is an ancient one, going back to 12th-century Japan. A bonsai is intended to capture all the beauty of a full-sized tree growing in the wild, but in miniature form. Harmony of all parts – the relationship of the branches to the trunk and the tree to its container – is very important.

Traditional bonsai trees are hardy species, such as maple, plum, cherry, juniper and pine, and must be grown outdoors. The latest trend is towards tender bonsai plants for growing indoors. These include bonsai pomegranates, weeping figs, olive trees, date palms and azaleas; all are available from specialist nurseries.

CHOOSING THE INGREDIENTS

Dyed-green, dried reindeer moss is used to form the tree's foliage. Order it from your florist or use natural, silver-grey dried reindeer moss and tint it green with either a broad-tipped magic marker, diluted food colouring or drawing ink. Another way of getting a similar effect is by wiring up sprigs of green-dyed broom bloom and inserting them into the foam block. This is more time consuming but the result is very effective, with the small blooms resembling delicate leaves.

Dried bun moss, in its natural grey-green colour, is used here to form the lawn beneath the tree. It can be ordered from your florist or you could collect it yourself from the wild and dry it in a warm place, such as an airing cupboard or on top of a boiler; alternatively, you could just leave it to dry out naturally in the display.

Traditional bonsai are usually under-planted with all-green carpeting plants, such as moss, mind-your-own-business, selaginella and occasionally the small pink flowers of sea thrift. To get the same effect, the small yellow achillea flowers were used in this display. Other plants which you could use for their different colour, texture and shape include: sprigs of dried gypsophila, dyed-pink broom bloom or glixia. Whatever flowers you decide to use, they should be very small; helichrysums, for example, would be far too large in relation to the tree.

CHOOSING THE BRANCH

Almost any forked branch may be used for this display. To be authentic, try to use a branch of a typical bonsai

SHAPING THE MOSS

To shape the reindeer moss to form the bonsai tree's foliage, carefully pull a large clump of moss apart into smaller pieces. Roll each of the smaller clumps individually between the palms of your hands gently forming them into balls. Continue making compact foliage balls with the remainder of the moss until you have enough to form your tree.

If you want the moss to retain its pliability treat it before shaping. with a mixture of half glycerine and half water. Heat it almost to boiling point, then let it to cool. Dip fresh moss in the solution and lay on absorbent tissue to dry.

species from the following list: pine, plum, cherry, juniper, hornbeam, beech, camellia, cotoneaster, dogwood, crab apple, elaeagnus, cryptomeria, chamaecyparis, maple, mulberry, pear, spruce, pyracantha, winter jasmine, holly, rhododendron or juniper. A gnarled bit of ivy root, twiggy oak branch or the oriental-looking branch of chaenomeles, or Japanese quince, would be ideal. If you do not have a garden, go for a walk in a park or in the country to search for suitable materials.

You could collect several unusual branches and build up a small collection of dried-flower bonsai trees, each with a distinct landscape and in a different type of pan. Arrange them together on a bookshelf or in a glass display case.

THE ACCESSORIES

Gravel and pebbles are available from builder's merchants, and larger DIY centres. Some tropical fish shops sell gravel and ornamental stones, but avoid unnaturally bright dyed gravel. Smooth, water-washed stones can be found on shingle beaches or in shallow streams. A small piece of driftwood found on the beach and used in place of the stones would give a natural touch. These materials are also available from tropical fish shops.

CHOOSING THE CONTAINER

Oriental shops and some of the larger garden centres stock ceramic or stoneware bonsai pans. Usually, they are glazed on the outside and unglazed on the inside; this is so that the clay of the pan can absorb water for the plant's roots. The pans come in round, oval, square, rectangular and hexagonal shapes, and in sizes ranging from 10cm (4in) across for miniature bonsai, to 60cm (2ft) or more. They can be flat or raised on feet, with straight or slightly curved sides, and protruding or rimless lips. Some are bowl-like and deep, while others are as shallow as saucers. They are all simple and unobtrusive so that the eye is not distracted and is able to concentrate on the beauty of the tree.

Glazes range from pale green and yellow to beige, grey, brown, dark blue and black, and some glazes are speckled attractively. Authentic bonsai pans are very simple, so if you do not want to go to the expense of buying one especially, you could use a small, brown-glazed casserole dish instead.

CHOOSING THE SETTING

Unlike a living plant which needs the correct light, heat and humidity to thrive, you can display this bonsai anywhere. Traditionally, it would be given a niche of its own so that its beauty could be contemplated without distraction. A plain background, such as a white or neutral wall or a simple bamboo screen would make a perfect setting. The surface where the tree stands should be equally plain; something modern, such as a white or black laminated surface, or a natural one, such as scrubbed pine or even slate, would be ideal.

1 1 rectangular Japanese ceramic pan 2 florist's dry foam block 3 scissors 4 strong transparent glue 5 1 large clump of dried bun moss 6 gravel 7 1 forked tree branch 20cm (8in) high 8 6 small stones 9 few sprigs of yellow achillea 10 1 bag of reindeer moss dyed dark green, a prong, and adhesive clay

MAKING
AN EVERLASTING BONSAI TREE

1 Cut a piece of florist's foam so that it is half the width of your rectangular container and about 2.5cm (1in) thick. The foam should sit about 1cm (½in) below the rim of the dish. Attach the foam to the base of the dish using a prong and some adhesive clay. Push the tree branch into the foam, to the right of the centre and towards the back of the display.

2 Cut two small blocks of florist's foam, one slightly longer than the other and both about 2cm (1in) thick. Place the longer piece on top of the two branches and glue it securely in position using strong transparent glue. Stick the smaller florist's foam block onto the lower branch. If necessary, fix the foam in position with florist's adhesive tape for added strength.

3 Break up the large clumps of reindeer moss into smaller pieces. (see box on page 47). Using the strong transparent glue, attach these pieces of moss to the florist's foam to act as foliage. Fill in the edges with more reindeer moss until you have achieved a rounded tree-top shape. Glue smaller clumps of moss to the underside of the foam.

4 Scrape off any excess soil from the bun moss, both for cleanliness and to remove insects. Fill in the left-hand side of the dish with about five or six large clumps of bun moss to create a natural landscape effect. Wedge them in tightly against one another and the sides of the dish to hold them in position. It should not be necessary to glue the moss in place.

5 Sprinkle about four or five handfuls of gravel over the foam base to conceal it. This will also help to anchor the tree in position. Lay six stones or pebbles around the base of the tree trunk to add to the desired landscape effect. Weathered stones with lichen or moss actually growing on them would help the display appear more authentic.

6 Lastly, to add a touch of colour, break off two or three sprigs of yellow achillea flowers. Trim the stems to 2.5cm (1in) long. Push them into the foam between the rocks and arrange them towards the right of the arrangement to balance the moss on the other side. As the key to a true bonsai is harmony, make sure everything is in proportion.

IMPROVING ON NATURE

Silk flowers bloom in luxuriant profusion nowadays. Whether you choose realistic or fantasy flowers, the choice is large

The craft of making silk flowers from special ribbons began in Japan in the 1960s when a Japanese lady, who lived near a textile factory, began making and later selling flowers made from their discarded materials. Enthusiasm for her flowers spread very quickly, first in Japan, then throughout the Far East; soon it was worldwide.

Today there is a wide range of fabric flowers and foliage – and even vegetables – available. The choice of material is usually between silk and polyester, the latter being less expensive and easier to keep clean but without the lustrous beauty of silk. Fabric flowers and foliage can be extremely lifelike, closely duplicating their natural counterparts. They can also be highly imaginative. You will find familiar flowers blooming in shades unknown in nature and others that make the best of all worlds, happily combining the buds and flowerheads of one plant with the foliage of another or even venturing further into the realms of fantasy and only owing their initial inspiration to the natural world.

It is not too difficult to make your own silk flowers. On the following

Silk flowers for widely different settings. An arrangement in soft, neutral shades (*opposite*) which will tone with many colour schemes; an elegant display of fantasy and lifelike flowers (*left*) and (*below*), a stunning conversation piece with silk flowers, fruit and vegetables

pages we give instructions for making hydrangeas and poppies using white silk and satin for flowers and foliage and hand painting them to achieve subtle gradations of colour. It is time-consuming pastime, but a most rewarding one.

Unlike fresh flower displays, silk flower arrangements can be displayed almost anywhere in the home. They are totally unaffected by sudden changes of temperature, to excessive heat and cold, to darkness or too much sunlight.

Silk flowers have one great advantage over fresh flowers in that they do not need watertight containers. This extends the range of possible receptacles enormously. If you make an arrangement in which the container is visible, it must be an integral part of your design; however, if it is hidden, it only needs to be of a suitable shape and depth. With fresh flower arranging, the weight of water in the container adds stablitity; but so that a silk flower display remains stable (and they can be top-heavy), use a heavy container, one with a broad base, or weight your chosen container down with stones.

SILK
HYDRANGEAS

Artificial silk flowers are often praised for their beauty as crafted objects, but not always for their likeness to the real thing. Our featured hydrangeas, in a subtle blend of pastel shades, have both qualities. Their realistic appearance is created by using the same colour tones and variations of texture as are found in nature. The techniques featured here evolved from the Japanese art of silk-flower making, and are quite simple to perform. However, the processes of cutting out, painting, and assembling each flower take time, so you should not aim to achieve more than a single flowerhead during your first session. For example, you will need to allow about half an hour for glued items to dry out thoroughly. Gradually, you can build up your hydrangea collection until you are able to achieve a generous, massed effect which will bring warmth and colour to any part of your home.

CHOOSING THE MATERIALS

Most of the raw materials, including the soldering iron and any toolheads you need to construct our featured flowerheads will be available in your local craft shop.

The flower petals are made from white silk and the leaves from white satin – both materials contribute to a professional finish. You should be able to get cheap silk and satin remnants from a fabric retailer or department store. In order to achieve the soft pastel shades required, always buy white

fabric and then handpaint it in the appropriate colours.

Coloured paper stem tape is an essential ingredient for silk flower designs. It is used to cover bare wires and fasten elements of the flowers together, and comes in a wide range of colours.

For glueing the stamens to the petals and the leaves to the stem, use a clear-based adhesive that will

become transparent as it dries, leaving the finished flower unmarked. These adhesives dry quickly once exposed to the air, so it is important to keep the lid on the pot, taking only a small quantity for immediate use. The double-sided sticky sheet and one-sided sticky foam are also necessary to assemble the flowerhead. If they are unobtainable in your area, stick the relevant parts together with adhesive.

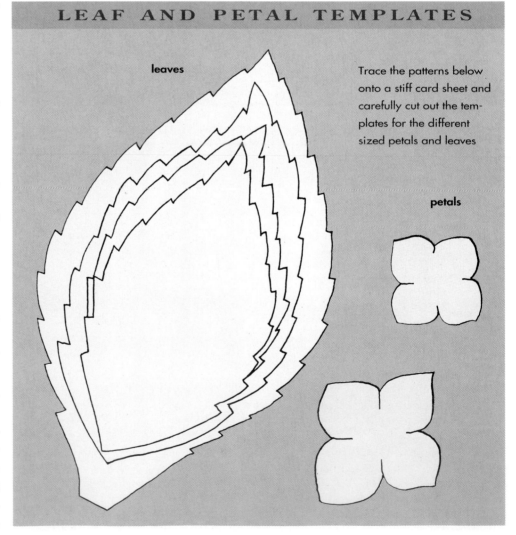

LEAF AND PETAL TEMPLATES

leaves

petals

Trace the patterns below onto a stiff card sheet and carefully cut out the templates for the different sized petals and leaves

CUTTING OUT THE FLOWERS & LEAVES

Hydrangea florets and leaves cut out and ready to make are available from craft shops but it is cheaper to make your own, either by drawing the shapes freehand onto the material or drawing round our petal and leaf tem-plates (left). Use a stiff card to make your templates and cut them to the dimensions given in the diagrams. For each hydrangea head you will need eight leaves and 45 flowers.

Place the four different-sized leaf templates on top of the satin material and draw round them with a pencil.

Recreate the generous form and fine colouring of hydrangea flowerheads using real silk and satin handpainted in pastel shades

Fold the satin material in half and secure at the edges with pins or clips. Cut carefully along the inside of each outline with sharp dressmaking scissors so that you have eight shapes, two of each leaf size. Always cut the material at a slant so that it is unlikely to fray and spoil the design.

Prepare the individual hydrangea flowers in the same way, placing the two different-sized petal templates on the white silk. Trace 23 star-shaped flowerheads, making an equal number of both medium and small-sized flowers, then fold the material into a double thickness and cut it out as before. Cut out all eight leaves and 45 petals at the same time so you can use the same paint mixture on all of them, for a second colour mixing may not match exactly.

A NATURAL EFFECT

The majority of silk flowers are made from specially designed flower-making ribbons, available from craft shops in a wide range of colours and textures. However, the ribbons do not have the delicate, crisp texture and natural sheen of real silk, nor do the pre-dyed colours contain the subtle tone variations that are achieved here with powder paints and water. You can vary the intensity of colour by applying water to gently lighten the tone on individual florets so that when combined into a single hydrangea flowerhead, they create a natural-looking gradation of colour. When painting the silk shapes, use a fresh area of blotting paper for each petal or leaf so that the excess paint is absorbed properly.

The use of soldering tools to mould the petals and imprint veins on the leaves adds to the authenticity of the final effect. However, take care not to apply the heated tool to individual petals or leaves for more than a few

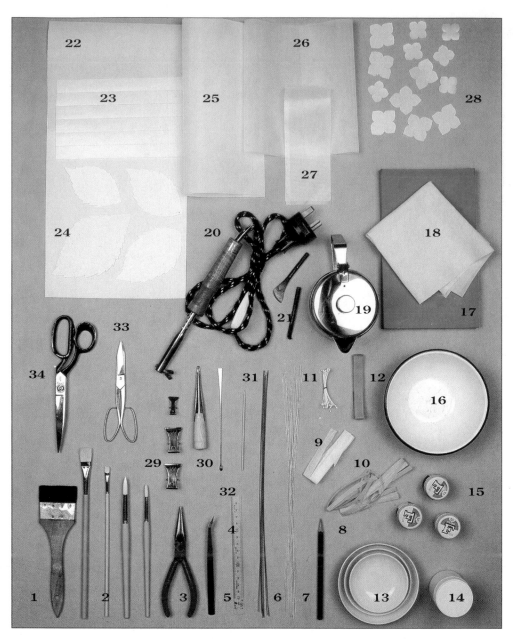

To make one hydrangea: **1** 1 large paintbrush **2** 4 small paintbrushes **3** wire cutters **4** tweezers **5** small ruler **6** taped stub wires **7** fine stub wire **8** pencil **9** white paper tape **10** pale green paper tape **11** 45 stamens **12** gutta-percha tape **13** small saucers **14** glue **15** blue/yellow/red powder paints **16** bowl **17** sheet of rubber **18** square of cotton **19** jug for water **20** soldering iron **21** 2 soldering iron tools **22** blotting paper **23** one-sided sticky foam **24** templates for leaves **25-27** 0.25sqm (¼ sq yd) each satin, fine silk & heavy silk **28** templates for petals **29** clips **30** spike **31** small spoon **32** bamboo stick **33** small scissors **34** dressmaking scissors, double-sided sticky sheet

seconds, otherwise the delicate fabric may burn. The tool you require for a particular task should always be attached to the iron before it is switched on. As soon as you have finished, turn off the iron and leave it to cool on its stand before attempting to remove the toolhead.

CHOOSING A VASE & SETTING

If you have only one or two hand-painted silk hydrangeas, you can still use them, either singly or as a pair, to striking effect in a tall, slender vase, where the beauty of each flowerhead can be appreciated. Once you have a number of hydrangea heads, you can

PAINTING
THE FLOWER PARTS

1 Mix the powder paints with water in three saucers. For the leaves, you will need blue and yellow for the base colour, red and blue for the centres, and blue, yellow and red for the outside shading. Use a separate brush for each colour. Dip the leaf into water and lay it flat on blotting paper. Paint it pale green, then paint a line of water down the centre.

2 Give the larger leaves another coat if necessary to make them a darker shade. Mix yellow, red and blue together and paint the dark green shade around the outside of each leaf. Darken the centre of the base of the leaf with the red and blue paint mixture. Press firmly with each brush stroke to make sure there are no air bubbles.

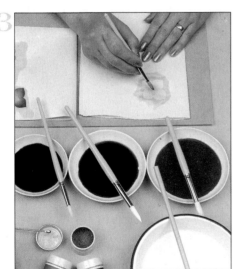

3 For the petals you will need to prepare; dark green, from blue, yellow and a little red; blue; mauve, from red and blue; and red. Dip the petal into the bowl of water. Place it flat on the blotting paper so that the excess moisture is absorbed. Dab a small amount of dark green paint in the centre of the petals Add a little water to lighten the petals if necessary.

4 Using a different brush for the three colours, dab blue, mauve and red around the edge of each petal. Add small amounts of water to wash the colours into each other so that they blend naturally. Make some petals dark and others light and try varying the colour combinations for each one. This will give the finished flowerhead a more natural appearance.

5 Lay a strip of heavy silk on a piece of blotting paper. Mix blue and yellow paints to make pale green. Using a thick brush and plenty of water, make wide, long strokes along the length of the silk to give it an even colour. This strip of silk is used to cover the flower stem. Use the pale-green mixture to paint the fine silk used to back the leaves.

6 Take a small bunch of white flower stamens purchased from a shop. Mix yellow paint and water. Using a small paintbrush, dab the yellow paint on each tiny stamen to make them pale yellow. You will need 45 stamens in all. Leave all the painted flower parts to dry thoroughly.

ASSEMBLING THE FLOWER

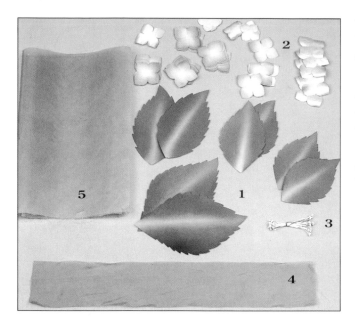

To assemble one hydrangea flowerhead you will need:

1 8 painted leaves
2 45 petals
3 45 stamens
4 painted strip of heavy silk
5 painted sheet of fine silk

display them effectively in many ways, such as in a large, circular pot or in a long, narrow, trough-like container. Green or white glazed china will complement the soft pastel shades of the petals, but a gleaming copper container, as used here, will provide a striking focal point.

Displayed en masse, the generous full-blown hydrangeas create a soft, welcoming touch. Mix the silk flowers with dried foliage for a fuller display. If you have an informal, country-style kitchen, hang a bunch of silk hydrangeas from the ceiling for a rustic effect.

Once you have found the perfect setting for your painted silk

1 When dry, stick down the eight leaves onto a double-sided, self-adhesive sheet. Trim round each leaf. Strip the backing from the sheet so that one side of the leaf is sticky. Place a 36cm (14½in) fine gauge stub wire along the middle of the underside of the leaf. The end of the wire must not reach the top of the leaf.

2 Place the leaf and wire diagonally across the grain of the fine silk so that the material does not fray. Trim round the edges of the leaf. The leaf is now covered on both sides. To form the stem, stick a piece of the painted pale green silk to sticky-sided foam. Cut out a narrow length, 4cm (1½in) long and stick to the top of the wire underneath the leaf base.

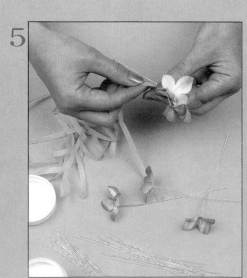

5 Use the bamboo stick to dab glue on the short length of stamen that sticks through the back of the flower. Stick a white stub wire to the stamen wire. Tape round the stamen and wire with gutta-percha tape to make one flower stem. Do the same with the other flowers. Bind together three stems to make a floret. Twist the outside petals slightly inwards.

6 Build up a round flowerhead using 15 florets with the darker flowers in the centre. Tape a short way down the flower stems with pale green paper tape held in place with glue. Push a stub wire into the bunch of stems. Tape all the way down the wire with white tape, held with glue. Stick a piece of silk-covered foam to the top of the stem to make it thicker.

hydrangeas, you probably will want to leave them on permanent display. While the initial impact is impressive, you may like to bring renewed interest to your arrangement by incorporating fresh flowers and foliage. For example, you can maintain a natural look all the year round, choosing fresh flowers, such as roses and carnations that are always available and will combine well with real hydrangea blooms. At other times of the year, mix seasonal fresh flowers and other artificial blooms with the hydrangeas.

COMPLEMENTARY COLOURS

Make a selection of colours that blend with the subtle pink, blue and cream shades of the painted silk flowers. Experiment with pink roses and scillas to set off the subtle shades of a pink hydrangea head. Blue scillas and pale yellow roses would combine well with a blue flowerhead. When choosing fresh foliage, pick substantial leaves that will support the weight and fullness of the hydrangea blooms, such as viburnum, or another large-leaved evergreen.

In mixed displays, although you will need a supply of water for your fresh flowers and foliage, it is not advisable to immerse the taped stems of the silk hydrangeas. Choose a large, broad-based container and place the fresh flowers and foliage in a small vase in the centre of it, surrounding the smaller vase with stones or other similar material into which you can insert a framing circle of attractive silk hydrangea stems.

SILK FLOWER AFTERCARE

Silk flower arrangements are usually left on display for lengthy periods so they will need regular cleaning. Dust collects quickly and, if left to gather on the painted surfaces of the leaves and petals, it may become sticky and difficult to remove. The ideal way to remove dust is to blow it off using a hairdryer, adjusted to a cool setting. Alternatively, you can also use a small, soft brush.

3 Use the sheet of rubber, covered with the cotton square for protection, as a work surface to mould the petals and leaves. Take the narrow soldering iron tool, run the iron down the centre of the leaf to form a groove on top of the wire midrib. Mark the veins on either side of the central groove in the same way.

4 Change the tool on the soldering iron for the blunt-ended one to shape the petals. Press the tool around the edge of each petal to make it curve gently. With the spike make a hole for the stamens in the centre of the petal shape. Cut the double-ended stamens in half and push one into the centre of each flower and glue in place.

7 Dab blobs of glue onto the stems of the two small leaves. Attach them on both sides of the main stem, just underneath the flowerhead, with white tape. Stick silk-covered foam round the main stem underneath the first two leaves. Turn the stem round and attach two of the next sized leaves with tape to face in the opposite direction.

8 Again, tape down the length of the main stem using white tape attached with blobs of glue. Cut another piece of silk covered with foam as before. Continue with the two pairs of larger leaves. Cover the remaining stem length with one long piece of foam. Finally, cover the sticky stem with a strip of pale green silk.

ORGANZA POPPIES

Fabric flowers are fun to arrange, last for ages and can be mixed with interesting combinations of both fresh and dried material. These colourful organza poppies are an economical alternative to ready-made silk blooms, especially since they can very easily be made from sales remnants and oddments left over from dressmaking found in your sewing basket .

DISPLAYING FABRIC FLOWERS

Part of the fun of making and arranging fabric flowers is that they do not have to look absolutely true to life. Start off by copying a real flower and as you become more confident move on to more unusual 'fantasy' blooms. Experiment by making exotic-looking flowers in unusual colours and shapes. There are all sorts of ways to display fabric flowers – not just in a vase or basket, but in a corsage or to decorate a hat for a special occasion.

CHOOSING THE FABRIC

If you have not had much practice at making your own flowers, the easiest materials to work with are the heavier ones such as linen. However, when finer fabric is needed for more delicate flowers – organza, silk, and satin are the best. The thin, almost transparent quality of organza makes it an ideal choice for delicate poppy petals.

TREATING THE MATERIAL

Unless the fabric has been pre-treated, you should prepare it for flower making with a starch and glue solution before cutting it out. As well as stiffening the fabric, this will prevent the edges from fraying and help to retain the shape of the petals and leaves, while keeping them looking fresh. (For details of how to treat the fabric, see box below.)

CHANGING THE COLOUR

If you want your fabric flowers to complement a particular colour scheme in your home and your material does not match, it can easily be dyed. Fabric

Show off your home-made poppies as most people like to see them – combined with a wealth of cereals reminiscent of a summer field. Display them in a rustic wall-hanging basket

dyes, or fabric paints are both widely available in a range of colours and are easy to apply. If you cannot find an exact match, then blend together a selection of different coloured paints. By mixing a darker colour into a

TREATING THE FABRIC

1 Pin the piece of organza completely flat on a clean, non-porous surface. Paint on the red dye in long, even strokes. Leave to dry overnight.

2 When the material is completely dry, iron out all the creases on a low heat until you have a smooth surface.

3 Blend a tablespoon of cold water into two tablespoons of ordinary household starch to make a smooth paste. Stir the paste into 175ml (6fl oz) of lukewarm water. Slowly bring to the boil, stirring constantly, and boil gently until the solution thickens. Remove from the heat and stir in a tablespoon of clear adhesive. Leave to cool. Pin out the material on a completely flat, non-porous surface. Brush the starch and glue solution evenly over the entire surface of the fabric. Dab off excess solution with a clean cloth and allow the fabric to dry overnight in a warm, well-ventilated place.

PETAL & LEAF TEMPLATES

Leaf

Petal

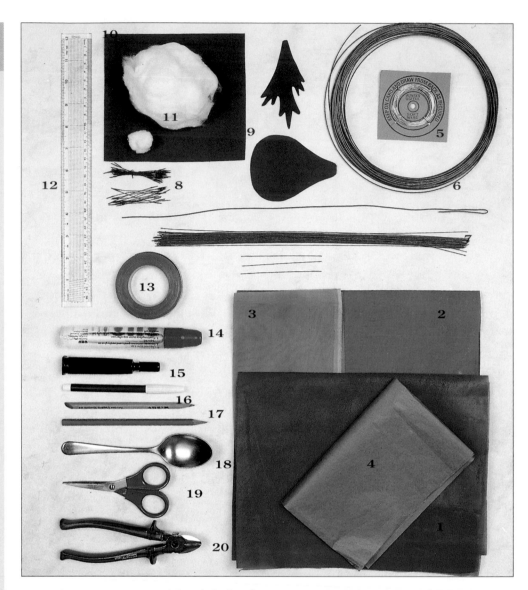

To make one poppy: 1 25cm (10in) red organza **2** 25cm (10in) green cotton or satin treated with starch or glue **3** small strip of pale green organza for the flower centre **4** 1 sheet of green tissue paper **5** thin-gauge reel wire for binding **6** 30cm (12in) stub wire **7** 3 lengths of stub wire cut to 6cm (2½ in) **8** 30 black stamens **9** templates **10** card **11** small ball of cotton-wool **12** ruler **13** florist's adhesive tape **14** clear transparent adhesive **15** thick black felt pen **16** black felt-tip or crayon **17** pencil **18** spoon **19** scissors **20** wire cutters

lighter one, or by diluting the colour, you can create different shades and hues to paint on the edges and in the curves of petals. To fix the paint and make the colour last longer, iron the fabric after painting it. Always dye material before applying the starch solution, as colour dyes will not hold evenly on treated fabric.

Artificial stamens are the all-important finishing touch. They are available from craft shops in a variety of colours and sizes, and most are made with 'pearl' tips. Stamens can also be made quite simply at home. Dip a length of cotton thread in starch, then hang it up to dry and harden. When it is quite dry, cut the thread into lengths of 6cm (2½in) and carefully dab a little glue at both ends. Allow it to dry and then paint on the appropriate colour – in this case, black for the poppies.

Give the petals realistic curves, hollows and creases by heating the back of a spoon or the edge of a spoon handle over a flame and drawing it firmly across the petal. Authentic bowl-shaped petals for flowers such as paeonies can be made by placing the organza or other material over a foam pad covered with cotton wool and pressing the hot bowl of the spoon firmly on the petal. Mark the indentations for the leaf veins with the back of a heated knife blade.

MAKING
AN ORGANZA POPPY

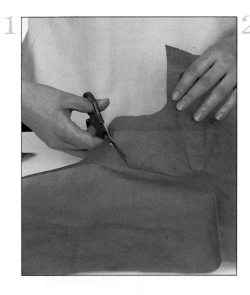

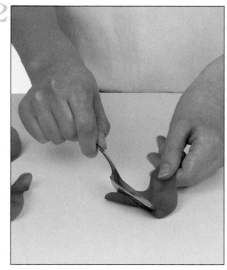

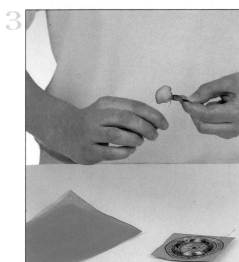

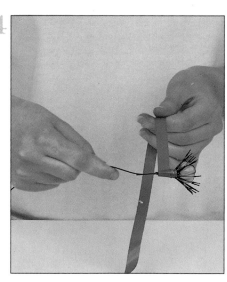

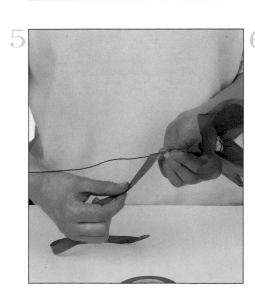

1 Trace the leaf and petal templates (pictured opposite) and cut out a master cardboard template of each of them. Place the petal template on the ready-prepared red organza (see box on page 59) and trace several outlines in pencil. Carefully cut out six petals for each poppy.

2 Iron the back of the petals to make them perfectly flat, then heat a metal spoon and draw it firmly across each petal to give a realistic curved shape. Colour in the bottom of the petal with a thick black felt-tip pen.

3 Bend back the top of a 30cm (12in) length of stub wire to form a hook. Glue a small ball of cotton wool to the top of the hooked wire to form the flower centre. Cover the ball with a small square of green organza. Bind the ends of the fabric to the stem with fine reel wire.

4 Wrap three lengths of wire covered with green adhesive tape over the top of the flower centre to secure it to the stem. Take 15 stamens, fold in half, and hang over a length of stub wire, wrapping the wire ends around the base of the flower centre. Evenly arrange the stamens. Secure the wires at the top of the stem with adhesive tape.

5 Arrange the petals and glue them one at a time around the flower centre, overlapping them slightly onto the calyx. Wrap a little crumpled green tissue paper under the petals to form the shape of the calyx. Cover the calyx with adhesive tape.

6 Outline two leaf shapes in pencil on the green cotton fabric and cut out. Mark the veins of the leaf lightly with a pen and shape the indentations with the back of a heated knife blade. Using fine wire attach each leaf to the stem about 5cm (2½in) below the poppy head. To complete your poppy, bind the entire stem with adhesive tape.

STRIKING
IN SILK

For a long time, silk flowers looked undeniably artificial. Even when seen from across a room, their unnaturally bright and solid colours, stiff stems and uniform size and shape made them a poor substitute for fresh flowers. Well all that's changed. Nowadays, modern manufacturing techniques, including photographic reproduction of the natural variations of leaf or petal colours onto fabric, have dramatically improved the appearance of silk flowers. Today, they not only look realistic, but more than that, they are also very beautiful objects in their own right.

Silk flowers last a lifetime, so always buy the best you can afford. As with any manufactured item, they do tend to vary in quality, and some are definitely cruder and less convincing than others. The term 'silk' is also sometimes loosely used to include polyester flowers. These, too, vary enormously. If you are on a limited budget, it is better to buy one or two top quality stems at a time and gradually build up a collection.

CHOOSING SILK FLOWERS & FOLIAGE

If you go to a large department store or an oriental shop that specialises in silk flowers, you'll be spoiled for choice. You can either follow the selection used here or choose alternative flowers and foliage to suit your colour schemes. To get a similar finished effect, buy roughly equal proportions of large and small flowers

and use approximately two thirds flowers to one third foliage, as shown. Whatever your final choice, make sure the stems are flexible enough to bend into curves, and strong enough to hold their shape once bent.

Three stems of pink lilies form the focal point of this display, but you could equally well choose white, cream, pale or deep yellow, orange or crimson shades instead, depending on your colour scheme. Make sure each stem has several open flowers and a few buds and that the flowers are widely, though not necessarily evenly, spaced apart.

A single spray of orchids in deeper pink emphasizes the colour scheme so, whatever colour lilies you choose, use the orchids to offset them.

Two types of small flower are used, both loosely based on nature. Part of the joy of silk flower arranging comes from the availability of such fantasy blooms – created for their own beauty and not restricted by what is found in the real world. The white, so-called 'seventh heaven' flowers are reminiscent of flowering cherries, although they wouldn't stand up to a botanist's scrutiny! The tubular-shaped, pale-pink 'star' flowers look like a mythical hybrid of miniature belladonna lilies and pink jasmine. Both the pink and white flowers form a delicate mass lightly concealing the lower stems of other material.

Silk foliage featured in this display includes variegated ivy and eucalyptus. You could use glycerined or air-

Perfectly framed in the window, where it acts as a colourful focal point on the dullest of days, this elegant silk flower arrangement tapers neatly at the tip, avoiding a wobbly or top-heavy look

dried eucalyptus instead. Glycerined eucalyptus is a deep reddish purple, which is perhaps not ideal for this particular colour scheme; the same is true of glycerined ivy, which is a rich tobacco brown. The third type of silk foliage used is the so-called 'watercress' – oddly named since it bears little resemblance to the salad plant of that name. Its lacy leaves contrast

CLEANING FLOWERS

Silk flowers do get dusty so whenever necessary wash them in a bowl of warm, soapy water. Rinse thoroughly, then hang somewhere warm and airy to dry. Make sure they are thoroughly dry before using or storing them, otherwise the stems may rust.

effectively with the more solid foliage of ivy and eucalyptus, and also make good filler material.

REAL OR FALSE?

Real plant material combined with silk flowers give variety and interest to a display. Here, dried poppy seedheads in their natural silvery-grey colour, and dried, curly willow complete with a few leaves, add a natural element to the display.

Dried, curly willow is sold at many florist shops, but if you are lucky enough to have a corkscrew hazel in your garden, you could use a few branches of that instead. Remember, though, that it grows much more slowly than willow, so choose your branches carefully and only cut as much as you need. Poppy seedheads are also available commercially in dyed and natural colours. You could also use love-in-a-mist seed pods.

CHOOSING
THE CONTAINER

The container used in this display is an inexpensive, modern hexagonal design. Made of glazed china, it is stylishly marbled in blue, grey and black to give a texture that is attractive, but not overwhelming. You could use a cylindrical or square container instead, providing it is straight sided and tall enough – say, 25-30cm (10-12in) high – to allow room for the lower stems to arch gracefully downwards. Transparent containers are not suitable as the stems of silk flowers are their least realistic looking part. Instead of the marbled effect, you could choose a white or a single colour vase to tone in with the colour scheme of your room. Avoid fiercely-patterned designs that would draw your eye away from the flowers and steer clear of colours that might clash with either the flowers or the setting.

1 1 bunch of watercress (artificial) **2** 1 bunch of small pink star flowers **3** 3 stems of white silk seventh heaven flowers **4** 3 pink silk lilies **5** 1 sprig of fake variegated ivy **6** 12-15 dried poppy seedheads **7** 1 spray of deep pink silk orchids **8** 3 stems of eucalyptus (artificial) **9** 2 stems of dried curly willow **10** florist's foam **11** wire cutters **12** floristry scissors **13** tall hexagonal-shaped vase

FITTING FOR
ANY LOCATION

This silk flower arrangement is beautiful enough to stand as a focal point anywhere in the house – on an entrance hall table, for example, or on a living-room or bedroom shelf, a landing windowsill or on a mantelpiece. Because it is a front-facing display, you may want to place it against a simple backdrop, such as a plain wall or a mirror.

Always remember that silk flower displays are the ideal choice for places that are unsuitable for fresh flowers: a draughty or unheated entrance hall, for example, or above a radiator. Silk flowers have the advantage of being impervious to heat, cold, chemical fumes and draughts, and will continue to give pleasure long after fresh flowers placed in a similarly awkward location would have faded and been consigned to the bonfire.

MAKING A SILK FLOWER
WINDOW DISPLAY

1 Cut dry florist's foam to fit snugly into the neck of the container. Press firmly into place, leaving 2.5cm (1in) of foam above the rim. Insert a large willow stem into one side of the foam block towards the front. Place another stem on the opposite side towards the back. These branches set the width of the display.

2 Use the lilies to set the height. Cut the tallest stem to 45-50cm (18-20in) using wire cutters. Bend the stem gently into a graceful curve and insert in the centre of the display. Turn the flowerheads slightly outwards. Cut the next stem slightly shorter, bend as before, and insert close to the first. Angle the third stem sideways.

3 Cut three eucalyptus stems to slightly different heights, leaving the tallest about 37.5cm (15in) long. Insert them tightly bunched and angled outwards from the centre to balance the shorter central lily stem. Cut three orchid flowers from the base of their stem, and insert them at the front to conceal the foam block.

4 Cut the sprig of ivy into individual leaves, again using wire cutters to get through the central wire core of the plastic stem. Make sure there is a short length of stem attached to each leaf for ease of insertion. Use the leaves to form a tight overlapping collar around the rim of the vase. This helps to conceal the foam block.

5 Insert three stems of seventh heaven – splayed out from a single point near the base – above the ivy. For a natural effect, cut the stems to different lengths and bend them so that they arch and curve gracefully downwards. Insert a tight cluster of 12-15 dried poppy seedheads of varying heights just off-centre.

6 Build up the central core, using shortened stems of 'watercress' foliage. Carefully inspect the display for any visible signs of the foam block and readjust or add more as camouflage, where necessary. Finally, cut the 'star' flower stems to varying lengths and insert randomly to fill any gaps.

FABRIC FANTASY

One of the beauties of silk flowers is that they can be used to provide the element of fantasy lacking in fresh florist's and garden flowers.

Think ahead and buy silk flowers in at least two colour combinations so you can create a variety of silk flower displays. Silk blooms in neutral colours, such as those in this arrangement, are a sensible buy since they look effective in a wide range of settings. Choose as many different shaped flowers within this limited colour spectrum as you wish, but avoid buying lots of different coloured flowers or you may find that it is difficult to form cohesive displays.

CHOOSING THE MATERIALS

This arrangement could be described as a study in white, while extra visual warmth is provided by cream, peach and pink-tinted silk and dried materials. Alternatively, choose white silk flowers with a hint of blue, mauve or green to transfer the colour accent from a warm to a cooler effect.

Most florist and interior design shops sell silk flowers grouped in colour ranges to help you co-ordinate your arrangements. This is particularly useful when making a monochromatic display such as our featured arrangement, where no less than six different types of silk flowers are used. Some do not resemble real flowers as closely as others, but this really is an advantage, since the main purpose of this display is to create an extravagant and eye-catching fantasy.

TAKING SHAPE

Shape and texture are both equally necessary when creating interesting monochromatic displays. Choose a range of flower sizes and types, mixing spiky blooms and flowers with large solid petals for contrast. Use sprays of flowers on flexible stems as well as single-headed varieties.

In our featured display, shape and textural interest are provided by large peach-tinted cactus dahlias, spider chrysanthemums – with their slender petals – and a peach-tinted, thread-like fantasy flower. A solitary spray of outsized, grey-green cymbidium orchids adds an exotic touch, as do the pink-tinted fruit blossom branches. Lastly, a fantasy flower that appears to be some kind of a cross between a large white tulip and a lily gives a finishing touch to the arrangement.

In general, the dried material is linear, in contrast with the cupped and flat forms of the silk flowers. Bear grass that has been dried and bleached by the sun is included in the display for its elegant, arching shape. Ti tree, in natural greenish-white, and bleached broom bloom are both used as an attractive way of disguising the stems of the silk flowers and adding extra bulk to the display. To accentuate the colour scheme, you could order these dried materials in matching dyed colours from a florist.

This arrangement is large and extravagant so you could include full heads of creamy-white pampas grass. If you grow pampas grass in the

These silk flowers range from the authentic to the fantastic, and are combined with ti tree, dried gypsophila, bear grass and broom bloom for linear contrast

SHAPING UP

Large silk blooms, such as those used in our featured display, are available from florists and from good department stores. The silk flowers come packed flat in long cellophane bags for transport and storage. To obtain natural looking or fantasy shapes from these blooms just bend their flexible stems and petals into different positions. These spider chrysanthemums can be curved or twisted into shape by winding each petal carefully but tightly around your forefinger. Continue until you have formed a natural-looking flower. To obtain the gently arching shapes of the silk cymbidium orchid stem and the blossom stems, gently manipulate the stems, bending them to form smooth curves.

garden, use it as a substitute for the ti tree or cypress. Pampas grass is also available at the florist in dyed colours.

CHOOSING THE CONTAINER

For our featured display, a large, old-fashioned jug that was probably part of a jug and washbasin set has been used as a container. Similar Victorian and Edwardian-style jugs can be found, reasonably priced, in antique and secondhand shops. As the pouring lip and jug handle are almost entirely concealed by the arching flowers and foliage, a traditional rounded vase could be used instead.

CHOOSING THE SETTING

Our featured arrangement has been placed so that it fills a large, sunny windowsill. This is particularly effective, as the sun highlights the silk flowers from behind and throws their unusual shapes into relief. It is one of the bonuses of artifical blooms that the heat from the sun on the windowsill does not affect them in the same way as it does fresh flowers and, as the colours are pale, any fading that occurs won't be noticed.

Alternatively, if you own a Victorian washstand, complete with jug and basin, why not use it to display this flower-filled jug. A nineteenth-century mahogany chest of drawers, especially a bow-fronted one, would make another attractive setting.

The arrangement featured here is constructed as a front-facing display, but it could be executed in the round by extending the bear grass around the outer edge of the jug, and by including another trailing spray of cymbidium orchids.

LOOKING AFTER THE DISPLAY

To keep the silk flowers in tip-top condition, gently blow the dust off the display from time to time with a hair

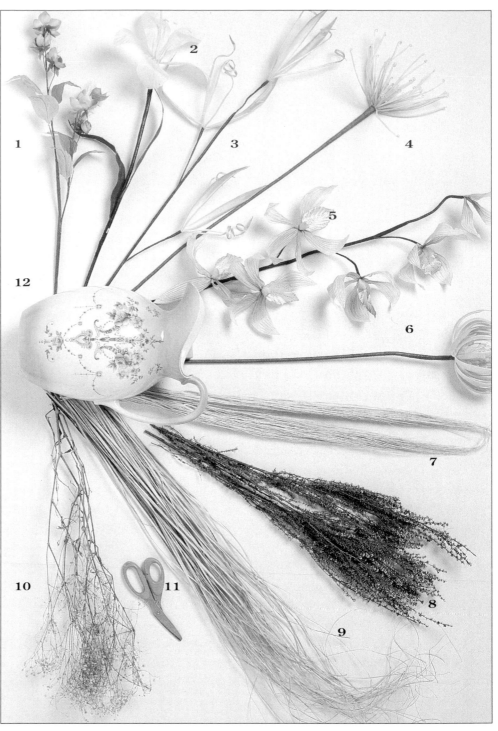

1 2 stems of pink silk fruit blossom **2** 6 stems of white silk lily flowers **3** 2 peach silk thread-like fantasy flowers **4** 3 peach spider chrysanthemums **5** 1 stem of white, silk cymbidium orchids **6** 3 peach silk dahlias **7** 1 bunch of dried bleached broom bloom **8** 1 bunch of ti tree stems **9** 1 bunch of dried bleached bear grass **10** 1 bunch of dried gypsophila **11** scissors **12** large jug

drier turned to a cool setting, and carefully remove any loose fragments of dried flowers that may have broken off. To enhance the arrangement for a special occasion, you could add an extra stem or spray of silk fantasy flowers, or perhaps even an exotic artificial bird with toning feathers; these are usually available from the same oriental shops that sell silk flowers.

CREATING
A LARGE JUG DISPLAY

1 Divide the bunch of bleached broom bloom into four or five. Trim the bottom 5cm (2in) off the stems. Fan out the small bunches around the outside of a large jug, allowing them to stand vertically. The stems are about one and a half times the height of the jug and establish the height and shape of the display. Allow the stem ends to cross one another for support.

2 Divide the bunch of ti tree into six and trim the stems, removing the bottom 5cm (2in). Intersperse the ti tree stems among the broom bloom. Use the stems to build up a front-facing fan shape. Take a single trailing stem of white orchids and curl the stem slightly so that it bends upwards. Position this stem in the front and to the right-hand side of the jug.

3 Curl the stamens of two thread-like fantasy flowers to make them less stiff. Trim the stems slightly. Place one on each side of the display towards the back, letting them stand higher than the broom. Trim the stems of eight white gypsophila sprigs by 5cm (2in). Insert at random among the flowers. Add about ten gypsophila sprigs to lighten the display.

4 Curl the petals of six white lilies outwards to make the flowerheads look more natural. Insert two blooms to the right and two to the left of the jug and two in the centre, making sure they all face forward. Next, curl the spiky petals of three chrysanthemums. Trim one chrysanthemum stem slightly shorter than the others and insert all three in the display centre.

5 Trim the stems of three silk dahlias to graduated heights. Arrange them in the centre of the display to create a focal point of large flowerheads. Next, bend two stems of fruit blossom to form elegant downward curves. Position the stems in the left of the jug so that they trail over the edge, breaking up the transition between the flowers and the jug.

6 Finally, take one bunch of dried bleached bear grass. Trim about 5cm (2in) off the stem ends and divide the bunch into four equal sized groups. Position the groups around the outer edge of the jug. Allow the stems to arch over the rim of the jug to break up its hard line. Check the position of the flowers before placing the arrangement in its intended location.

SILK STILL LIFE

This remarkable display contains a combination of realistic and fantastic material to create a conversation piece for any setting. The fanciful and intriguing components demand a bold and imaginative approach.

SILK OR POLYESTER
Polyester is a popular fabric for this type of decoration, as it less expensive than silk and easier to keep clean with a few dabs from a damp cloth. For this display either silk or polyester flowers, fruit and vegetables can be used as long as they are all of equally good quality and their appearance is appealing to the eye.

This arrangement has a predominantly light pastel colour scheme combined with the sharply contrasting touches of blue-black and bright yellow. Alternatively, you could choose a rich orange and red scheme, using fabric tiger lilies, tomatoes, carrots, oranges and apples; or a vibrant blue and violet scheme, based on blue-black grapes, purple plums, beetroot, delphiniums, cornflowers, deep purple anemones and perhaps even a startling red cabbage.

CHOOSING THE FLOWERS

There is a huge range of fabric flowers available, all of which are suitable to mix with material fruit and vegetables. You can follow the selection shown here or opt for a completely different one. For contrast try to include some large, trumpet-shaped flowers, tall flower spikes and branches of small, delicate flowers.

Pale pink and white lilies are the largest flowers used in the arrangement featured here. Real lilies come in all colours except blue, and fabric lilies even rectify this omission, so you should have no trouble finding material for your chosen colour scheme.

In nature, pussy willow is a large shrub or small tree with rigid, upright branches – quite distinct from the popular weeping willow. Here, an excellent fabric version combines the furry buds of the pussy willow with the elegant, curving branches of the weeping willow.

The large flower spikes covered in pink blossom are other examples of artistic licence. They combine the density of a hybrid delphinium with the flower shape of hollyhock, stock and sweet pea with a touch of orchid.

The tiny sprays of black-centred pink flowers are similar to rush flowers, but, again, make no attempt to copy nature exactly. They add a delicate lace-like quality reminiscent of gypsophila or sea lavender, and fabric gypsophila could be used instead.

CHOOSING THE FRUIT & VEGETABLES

Fabric fruit and vegetables are available from some gift shops, large department stores, oriental shops (since most are manufactured in the Far East), florist shops and major gar-

den centres. Any shop that carries a large selection of silk flowers is also likely to have a reasonable selection of silk or polyester fruit and vegetables.

In this display, silk turnips, cos lettuce, purple grapes, green apples and bananas are used. The choice is entirely subjective – you could use any combination of lemons, limes, white grapes, red apples, peaches, apricots, or rhubarb. The cos lettuce is used in the traditional role of ordinary, ornamental foliage: as contrasting colour and form for the flowers. Fabric spinach, cabbage or even radiccio could be used instead, but try to include some green material.

For an authentic tropical effect, use a huge silk pineapple complete with its tuft of spiky leaves. Continue the exotic theme by combining it with one or two fabric versions of the extraordinary flowers of the bird-of-paradise flower, *Strelitzia reginae*.

Again, the final effect of the arrangement depends on the quality of the ingredients. For a subtle still life in toning beiges and browns, wooden fruits and vegetables could be used, perhaps teamed with glycerined foliage, seed pods and dried flowers for a rich contrast.

If you are good at sewing and have enough time, you can make your own fabric fruit out of polyester, felt, or even fabric to tone with your upholstery or drapes. Craft sections of paper pattern catalogues sometimes have patterns specifically for fabric fruit and vegetables, as do some soft-furnishing books and magazines.

CHOOSING THE CONTAINER & RIBBON

In the display featured here, a wicker picnic basket is used. The raised flaps

Humour has a rightful place in flower arranging, provided it's not overstated. In this formal, very dignified setting the fantasy flowers, fruits and vegetables add light relief

RAFFIA BOWS

Take 1m (3ft) of ribbon and unravel it widthways. Cut a second length, 10cm (4in) long, but do not unravel this as far. Loop the first ribbon three times and hold it firmly where the loops cross. Attach to the handle with the second piece of raffia ribbon.

add an angular touch, but you could use an ordinary basket with a central handle. To take the freshly picked fruit and vegetable theme even further, choose an old-fashioned wicker garden trug but, if you are using one from a garden shed, clean and dry it well first. Since some of the fruits and vegetables used are wired to the outside of the container, a basket with a loose, open weave will be your best choice. A handle is not absolutely necessary but it does add height and will look attractive with pussy willow entwined around it.

The broad crêpe-paper ribbon is a relatively new product for flower arrangers. Sold in a compact form on

SECURING IMITATION MATERIALS

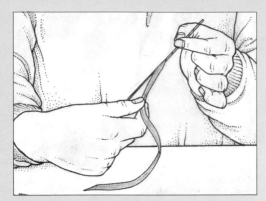

To ensure that the stub wire securing the fabric fruit and vegetables to the basket does not rust and mark the material, cover the wire with gutta-percha tape. The gutta-percha tape also makes the wire look more attractive.

Hold the tape against the wire and stretch it taut. Revolve the wire so that the tape wraps around itself in a spiral down the wire. The moisture and warmth of your hand should bind the tape to itself and to the wire.

Place a wire about 20cm (8in) long covered in tape around the middle of the fruit – in this case a banana. Make sure that the banana lies in the middle of the wire and twist the wire ends together. Use the rest of the wire to secure the fruit to the basket weave.

1 3 silk lilies **2** 5-6 stems of silk pussy willow **3** 3 silk hollyhocks **4** 3 sprays of silk sea lavender **5** 2 material bananas **6** 1 material cos lettuce **7** 3 silk turnips **8** 1 bunch of material grapes **9** 3 material apples **10** picnic basket **11** dry florist's foam **12** scissors **13** raffia paper ribbon **14** green gutta-percha tape **15** short stub wires **16** transparent glue **17** prong

round reels, it opens out like an accordion, to produce a ruched, fabric-like effect. It is available in a range of colours from the gift-wrap section of large department stores, and from some gift shops. Wide satin ribbon, toning with the colour scheme of the display, could be substituted or, for an unusual touch, try a plain or paisley silk scarf in a toning colour knotted round the handle.

The visual references to food in this arrangement make a kitchen the natural setting for this display. However, if your kitchen is too small or cluttered, a dining-room table or sideboard would be just as good, and there is less risk of cooking ingredients staining the display.

To extend the theme of the display, you could scatter a few fabric strawberries or apples near the display, or put them on a plate, as a temptation to guests. Alternatively, fix several little sprigs of green and black grapes to the handle. You could also include some real fruits and vegetables in the display among the imitation varieties to blur the distinction between illusion and reality even further.

FABRIC CARE

Fabric flowers, fruit and vegetables last indefinitely and so are bound to get dusty. If they are not sold with washing instructions, they can generally be immersed in a sink full of lukewarm water and washing powder designed specifically for delicate fabrics. This will get rid of the worst of the dirt and dust. Rinse the material fruit and vegetables thoroughly in clear, lukewarm water and, if possible, hang upside down to dry. For decorations that cannot be washed, blow off the dust with a hairdryer.

ASSEMBLING
YOUR FANTASY FLOWERS

1 Place a block of florist's dry foam in the basket. If necessary secure it in position with transparent glue. Wire both flaps of the basket lid to the handle by threading a piece of wire through each flap and twisting the wires securely around the basket handle. Cut off the excess wire and tuck the sharp ends into the basket lid.

2 Wrap a wire around a fabric banana (see box on opposite page). Push the ends of the wire through the weave in the right-hand corner of the basket. Twist the wires together inside the basket and cut off the ends. Wire a second banana and place it directly below the first. Wire the tops of the turnips and attach two to the lid and one to the handle.

3 Bend each lily stem to form an exaggerated 'S' bend and insert three stems of different lengths to the front right corner of the foam so that the shortest is tucked inside the basket. Cut the leaves from a stem and use them to hide the foam. Cut three 'hollyhock' stems to different lengths and place at the back right-hand side of the basket.

4 Hide the wire around the middle of the bananas by placing the bunch of grapes so that it trails out of the basket on the left-hand side of the display. No wiring is required, just insert the stem of the grapes into the foam. Fill in the rest of the left-hand side with three green apples and the cos lettuce. Wire the fruit and vegetables, if necessary.

5 Twist about five or six long silk pussy willow stems around the basket handle. Start from both ends of the handle and wind the stems around it until they meet in the middle. Where the wires meet you can use a couple of flowerheads to hide the mechanics. Group more pussy willow at the back right-hand side of the display to balance the flowers.

6 Construct a large raffia ribbon bow for the basket handle (see box on page 71 for details). Add three sprays of sea lavender to the front right-hand side of the display to balance the other items and to fill in any gaps in the grouping. Ensure that the foam block is completely covered. View the basket from all angles and adjust where necessary.

PUTTING
ON THE RITZ

Try introducing a touch of theatre into your home with a silk flower fantasy. Transform a fancy-dress top hat and a few simple silk flowers into an everlasting magical display that evokes all the romance of an era now long since gone.

This arrangement would make a splendid floral centrepiece for a party. As it comprises silk flowers and foliage, you can take the display apart quickly and rearrange the various items in a less dramatic but equally attractive way once the party is over.

The project is front-facing, and consists of black and white silk flowers and foliage. It is built up in an asymmetrical triangle on a concealed block of florist's foam and displayed in a silk top hat. The hardest part of the project is getting hold of a top hat. If you are unable to find one, then adapt the display to suit a hat of your choice.

BLACK AND WHITE

Pure white flowers are abundant in nature, and white is especially effective for attracting dusk or night-flying insects. Many coloured species have produced a white form, usually indicated by the term *alba* or *albus* after the specific name.

There are no pure black flowers growing naturally. A few come quite close – the black tulip, 'Queen of Night'; the hardy herbaceous perennial mourning geranium, *G. phaeum*; the velvety black and green widow's iris, *Hermodactylus tuberosus*; the vio-

las 'Mollie Sanderson' and 'Bowles Black'; and the hellebore 'Ballards Black'.

AN EVOCATIVE COMBINATION

Black and white has both modern and old-fashioned design connotations. Black and white interiors and clothes are at the height of contemporary fashion, yet black and white television programmes and films hark back to the first half of the twentieth century. This black and white display is contemporary in feeling, with the top hat providing a hint of nostalgia. Wherever necessary, the green foliage is sprayed black, and the green stems are taped with white gutta-percha, to conceal unwanted colour.

ALTERNATIVE CONTAINERS

An upturned black bowler, with blue tacky clay fixed to the top to keep it from tipping over, would be an alternative container. In addition, bowlers are easier to find than top hats.

For a more contemporary design, you could use a black or white cylindrical ceramic vase, a simple marble vase, a clear glass cylinder or cube vase. A cheaper alternative could be to cover a simple terracotta flower pot with several coats of gloss paint.

A stiff, red felt Moroccan fez could be upturned and used as a container for a red and white, or red, white and black scheme. You may find one in an antique shop or at a fancy-dress hire department.

CHOOSING THE FLOWERS & FOLIAGE

Silk flowers are used here, but good quality polyester flowers also would be suitable. Alternatively, feather flowers would make a display full of fantasy and glamour. Oriental shops, department stores, gift shops and larger garden centres generally have a good choice of artificial flowers and foliage.

Two enormous, larger-than-life white anemones are featured. They catch the eye immediately, in contrast to the more lifelike flowers. Huge, outsized silk poppies could be substituted, or hand-made silk cabbage roses or gardenias, bought from a millinery department. Attach them to false stub wire stems for added height. Slender white silk fantasy flowers offer linear movement to the display. You could use white silk spider chrysanthemums instead, or sprays of white silk orchids, on extended false stems if necessary.

The black silk paeonies have soft, grey foliage. If the only paeonies you can find have green foliage, strip it off or spray paint the leaves.

A bird of paradise (strelitzia) leaf, sprayed black, adds a strong vertical element. An artificial or dried black-sprayed aspidistra leaf or large palm leaf would make good alternatives.

One stem of silk pilea leaves is broken into several sprigs, which are used to fill out the base of the display. Like strelitzia, the pilea is sprayed

This black and white design comprises silk materials in a top hat. White gutta-percha tape and black spray paint hide the green stems and leaves

SPRAYING LEAVES & FLOWERS

To change the colour of the flowers and foliage you can spray them with a wide variety of paints.

Car paint spray dries very quickly and, if used lightly, gives a matt finish, although matt or gloss sprays from hardware shops have better covering capacity .

Decorative sprays bought from florists are attractive when used lightly, although thick layers look artificial. Metallic sprays add a glamorous sparkle.

Most paint sprays should be kept away from direct heat. They are best used at room temperature and should be shaken thoroughly before use to ensure even paint distribution. To prevent the nozzle clogging after use, turn the tin upside-down and spray until no more comes out. White spirit will remove any clogged or dried paint on the nozzle.

Before spraying, dust the silk leaves and open out the flower petals. Protect your work surfaces with several layers of newspaper and open the windows to provide adequate ventilation; spray paints can make you feel light-headed if used in confined areas. Spray an even coat of two or more paint layers, if necessary, allowing each layer to dry thoroughly before applying the next.

black to match the colour scheme. Any small-leaved silk foliage could be substituted; for example, silk ivy, Boston fern or tradescantia.

CHOOSING THE ACCESSORIES

In the top-hat display, black and white plastic chips are used to conceal the dry florist's foam block, once all the flowers and foliage stems are in place. Plastic chips, in black, white and various colours, are available from some florist shops and sundries wholesalers. You can order them if they are not immediately available.

FINDING ALTERNATIVES

You could use pure white or black gravel from a tropical fish shop, or black or opaque white marbles. Otherwise, tuck one or two inexpensive black or white, silk or chiffon scarves into the spaces between the stems.

A gentleman's walking cane, white kid gloves and pocket watch act as accessories to the main display, harking back to the elegant charm of Fred

DRIED FLOWER ALTERNATIVES

If you are unable to find suitable silk flowers for use in the display, transform a dried flower or seedhead by spraying it black or white.

Huge ornamental allium or leek seedheads make stunning fantasy flowers. *Allium giganteum*, with its 15cm (6in) wide, globe-shaped flowerheads is particularly dramatic.

Dried bamboo stems, with the leaves vertically shredded, could be sprayed white to look like the white fantasy flowers featured in this display. Chinese lanterns, sprayed black or white, or in alternating colours, and cut into short sprigs, would make good substitutes for the silk pilea leaves.

1 1 black silk paeony **2** 2 stems of white silk fantasy flowers **3** 1 stem of black-sprayed silk pilea plant **4** 2 giant white silk anemones **5** 1 black-sprayed silk bird of paradise leaf **6** handful of black and white plastic chips **7** top hat **8** block of dry florist's foam **9** white gutta-percha tape **10** scissors or wire cutters

Astaire. Inexpensive black and white feather boas, old theatre or cinema tickets, programmes or tiny opera glasses, would all help to create an image of the thirties.

A black and white setting, such as a chequerboard linoleum floor and white walls, perfectly suits the black and white theme, but it may not always be possible. If it suits the decor of the room, place a framed poster for an old black and white movie on the wall behind the arrangement. A sixties-style black and white, geometric op art poster or print would be suitable for a more modern arrangement.

DISPLAYING
SILK FLOWERS IN A TOP HAT

1 Push a block of dry florist's foam inside the hat. Most silk flowers come with stems that have already been covered with green tape. To keep to the black and white theme, use florist's white gutta-percha tape, winding the tape down the full length of each part of the stem of the white fantasy flower. Insert the stem vertically in the middle of the foam.

2 Silk bird of paradise leaves are usually dyed vivid green. To match the other flowers in the black and white display, spray-paint the leaf and stem black with several coats of paint to produce an even colour. Insert the bird of paradise leaf vertically in the middle of the foam, in front of the white silk fantasy flower. Bend the side bloom so it is visible.

3 Often black silk paeonies are sold with ready-dyed grey leaves that harmonise with the black and white flowers. If not, spray-paint them to match the rest of the design. Cut the paeony stem so that it stands 25cm (10in) lower than the top point of the central fantasy flower. Insert the paeony stem vertically, in front of the bird of paradise leaf.

4 Strip the leaves from the two large white silk anemones. Conceal the green stems by covering them with white tape. Place one flower facing forwards in the centre of the display, at the same height as the lower black paeony flower-head. Cut the stem of the other white bloom and insert it to stand below the first, with the flowerhead facing to the front.

5 Insert one more tall fantasy flower, again with the stem concealed with white tape. Cut the stem short and place it behind the silk anemone. Break up the branch of black silk pilea into four or five smaller stems. Insert them around the brim of the hat. Bend two of the side stems to curl upwards slightly. Bend the remaining stems so that they curl downwards.

6 Apart from the bushy pirea stems, there is no filler material to disguise the foam block when the display is viewed from above. Cover up any exposed patches of foam by sprinkling an even layer of small black and white plastic chips over the surface. If the chips are made from glossy plastic they will add some extra sparkle and glamour to the arrangement.

MIXED MEDLEYS

Take a fresh approach
and combine potted
plants with cut
flowers; fresh flowers
with dried flowers;
and artificial berries,
fruit and nuts
with their natural
counterparts

In this chapter we have devised a series of projects which take a novel approach to flower arranging by combining a series of unlikely materials to spectacular effect. They provide a splendid chance for you to let your imagination run riot, and to see what decorative triumphs you can achieve.

Fresh and dried flowers are not usually combined in the same arrangement since the bright colours of fresh flowers tend to set the subtle, muted tones of dried flowers at a disadvantage, giving them a faded look. However, in the hanging basket display on page 85, dried hakea foliage is combined with chrysanthemums and other fresh flowers. In this case, the grey hakea foliage is so large and dramatic that its impact is in no way diminished.

The *pot-et-fleur* is a French idea, as its name implies, and a very clever one. It describes an arrangement which combines potted plants with fresh cut flowers and foliage. Arrangements of this sort can last a considerable length of time if you

Three sumptuous displays. *Opposite*, an autumnal everlasting tree with real and artificial pods and berries. *Left*, a fragrant *pot-et-fleur*, and (*below*), an informal arrangement with fresh flowers and leaves and artificial fruit

choose long-lived pot plants. The cut flowers are replaced as and when necessary; you can use the same type of flowers each time or ring the changes if you prefer.

When combining fresh and dried flowers and foliage, it is most important that the stems of the dried material do not get wet, otherwise they will rot. To prevent this, bind them with waterproof gutta-percha tape. Porous containers must be waterproofed too if they are to hold saturated foam, plant pots or water containers. The easiest way is take a plastic shopping bag or dustbin liner and cut it to fit.

Our dried-flower tree has both real and artificial berries and nuts. In this case combining the natural and the artificial means a greater variety of materials to work with, giving additional textures and colours. This also applies to the *Fruits of the Forest* display. However, in this case, there is the very practical bonus that you can avoid using real berries which might stain any fabrics with which they come into contact.

SPRING
POT-ET-FLEUR

Most of us spend a lot of time in the kitchen, preparing meals and doing housework. Here's a way to get on with the chores in the presence of colourful spring flowers and foliage. Yellow and blue is an especially spring-like combination of colours which is found in many gardens during the spring months.

Pot-et-fleur is a French term that is used to describe an arrangement which combines potted plants, cut flowers and foliage. With long-lived house plants, such as Boston fern, ivy or African violet, you can keep the general framework of potted plants intact and replace the cut flowers with fresh ones, when necessary. With reasonable care, you should get at least two weeks' worth of pleasure from short-term flowering pot plants, such as polyanthus.

WOODEN BOWL CARE

To get the maximum life from a wooden bowl, try to keep it away from water. Whether you use it for flower arranging, salads, or both, a wooden bowl that is frequently washed can split. Instead, wipe it thoroughly clean with a dry cloth or paper towel after each use. An occasional rub with vegetable oil, such as olive or safflower, improves the appearance of the wood, as well as keeping it in good condition. If you have to wash a wooden bowl, avoid using harsh detergents and do it as quickly as possible. Make sure it is thoroughly dry before storing.

CHOOSING THE CUT FLOWERS & FOLIAGE

The size of a *pot-et-fleur* is determined by the container. Depending on your budget and the space available, your display can be as large or as small as you wish. If you want to make a miniature *pot-et-fleur*, buy the young plants known as 'tots', in 4cm (1½in) pots, which are usually sold for bottle gardens. Whatever size you choose, the display should look generously full, and the potted plants and cut material should blend so that you cannot see the flowerpot rims.

Though some fresh material from the florist is used in the *pot-et-fleur*, much of the display's charm comes from the informal collection of sprigs of garden shrubs and flowers. Make the best of whatever is to hand; an ordinary garden can easily supply all the material in this arrangement.

If you don't have a garden, show the picture of our featured display to your florist for reference. The florist should be able to sell you a similar combination of flowers and foliage.

Guelder rose and grape hyacinths are popular spring flowers available at the florist. Guelder rose is also known as the snowball bush, since its young, green flowerheads turn pure white when they mature. As an alternative, you can use mop-head hydrangeas. To prevent hydrangea heads wilting, condition them by submerging the flowerhead and the stem under water for several hours or overnight, before adding them to your arrangement.

Grape hyacinths are popular, hardy garden bulbs, so grow some of your own or buy grape hyacinths from the florist. They are inexpensive and have long, thick stems that are ideal for flower arranging. Grape hyacinths come in white, too, but they are rarely grown commercially. Scillas or chionodoxas could be substituted. Both are dwarf, spring-flowering bulbs, with spikes of flowers in a range of bright and soft blues, as well as white. Brightly coloured wallflowers are one of the delights of a spring garden, but they are rarely seen at the florist. Grow them in your own garden, or beg a few from a friend or neighbour.

CONDITIONING BRUNNERA

Brunnera is an old-fashioned, hardy herbaceous perennial, also known as Siberian bugloss. Its flowers are similar to forget-me-nots, which are a close relative. However, brunnera leaves are much larger than forget-me-not leaves and they increase in size throughout the summer. To keep brunnera flowers fresh, dip the cut stems in boiling water for a couple of seconds, follow this with a long drink of water. Forget-me-not or lungwort (*pulmonaria*) flowers could be used instead.

Skimmia is a tough, evergreen shrub that grows in shady spots in many gardens. The bright red berries of the female plants provide a colourful touch in autumn and winter. Similarly, you could use laurustinus, small-leaved laurel or evergreen euonymus foliage.

SMALL-LEAVED PLANTS

There are many different hebe species and cultivars. Choose a small-leaved type, in scale with the other fresh materials in the *pot-et-fleur*. Hebes usually flower in summer or autumn, but occasionally they bloom at other times of the year.

Rosemary is an old-fashioned, slow-growing herb. Often, you can buy sprigs from a greengrocer or super-market but they may be a little shorter than the rosemary featured in this display. Upright branches of juniper

or other conifers could be substituted, or long stems of box. The most unusual items are cut stems from a flowering indoor jasmine, *Jasminum polyanthum*. Its twining stems and fern-like foliage add a linear grace to the arrangement, while the delicate flowers are deliciously scented. You could buy one or two tiny pots and add them with their root-balls intact. To avoid overcrowding the root space, substitute cut sprigs of ivy for the pot-ted ivy. Alternatively, use asparagus fern or broom.

This *pot-et-fleur* captures the vitality of spring. Rooted ivy and polyanthus are combined with cut sprigs of wallflower, rosemary, hebe, skimmia and brunnera, guelder roses and grape hyacinths

Finally, sphagnum moss plays a vital role by hiding the florist's foam, retaining moisture and providing a unifying cover of greenery. If you live near a wood, you should be able to find a lovely mixture of mosses. You could also use bun moss.

WATERPROOFING YOUR WOODEN BOWL

1

2

3

1 Line the bowl with a clean plastic bag, arranged so that it covers the surface completely, and fasten in place with florist's adhesive clay.

2 Soak two florist's foam blocks, then cut them into three rectangular blocks 5cm (2in) thick and three or four pieces about 2.5cm (1in) thick. Wrap the base of each block in plastic, leaving the surface uncovered. Now you are ready to place the blocks in position.

3 Once you have decided on the position of each block, secure them using a prong and blobs of adhesive clay, then add the potted plants.

1 4 wallflower stems **2** 2 hebe foliage stems **3** 6 sprigs of brunnera **4** 1 bunch of grape hyacinths **5** 1 bunch of skimmia **6** 6 sprigs of rosemary **7** 4 sprigs of indoor jasmine **8** 4 guelder roses **9** 2 pots of yellow and blue polyanthus **10** 2 pots of ivy **11** 1 bag of sphagnum moss **12** 1 plastic dustbin liner **13** 1 large wooden bowl **14** 2 blocks of florist's foam **15** floristry knife **16** floristry scissors

CHOOSING THE POT PLANTS

Choose cheap and cheerful pot plants. You can combine whatever pot plants you think go well together, but if you want them to last, try to choose plants that like conditions similar to those that you are providing.

Yellow and blue polyanthus are shown, but polyanthus come in a rainbow of colours; some with contrasting centres, or 'eyes'; others with lacy, contrasting edges to the petals. You could use three identical or three different polyanthus plants, for a multicoloured effect. Since polyanthus are popular spring bedding plants, a garden centre may have a wider selection than a flower shop. Pot plants of double daisies, Italian bellflower, *Campanula isophylla*, or calceolaria could also be used to good effect.

Variegated ivy comes in many

ARRANGING CUT FLOWERS AND FOLIAGE

1 Prepare the wooden bowl (see box opposite) and place the polyanthus and the ivy plants between the foam blocks. Allow the ivy to trail over the edge of the bowl. Begin filling out the display around the edge of the bowl. Trim pieces of skimmia and hebe foliage to a length of 12.5cm (5in). Insert them into the foam around the outer edge of the bowl to add texture.

2 Cut several sprigs of rosemary to different lengths, down to about 20cm (8in) long. Place five sprigs in decreasing height from the centre down the left of the display. Trim the guelder roses to 10cm (4in) long and position the full florets around the rosemary to the right, left and back of the bowl. Place three or four more sprigs of skimmea in this central area to fill it out.

3 To add width, insert three or four trailing pieces of jasmine about 20cm (8in) long to the right of the arrangement. Balance this with two more stems on the opposite side. The white flowers help to lighten the display and add fragrance. Position 20cm (8in) lengths of trailing ivy stems around the back of the bowl. Note the natural curve of the stems.

4 Cut five or six stems of brunnera and wallflowers to a length of 25cm (10in) and 15cm (6in) respectively. Remove the leaves from the stem ends. Place the brunnera towards the centre left of the bowl. Add three to five stems at a time for greater impact. Add the wallflowers individually to make a cluster of five or six stems, slightly to the right of the centre.

5 Cut eight grape hyacinth stems to a length of 25cm (10in). Remove the foliage from each stem. Cluster all eight in the centre of the bowl in front of the rosemary, to build up the highest point in the display. Add some grape hyacinth stems in decreasing heights down the left and right-hand sides of the bowl to bring colour down through the display.

6 Finally, place about five handfuls of moss over the foam and pots in the display to disguise the mechanics and to keep in the moisture. Gently lift up the plant material and tuck the moss over the foam and plant pots. If you wish to secure the moss in position, use 5cm (2in) lengths of stub wire, bent into a hairpin shape, to pin it onto the florist's foam blocks.

sizes, colours and leaf shapes, with yellow, grey, creamy-white or even crimson coloured markings. There are also several attractive cultivars of all-green ivy, with deeply-lobed or frilled leaves. Again, choose a small-leaved variety, to keep in proportion with the rest of the delicate display.

CHOOSING THE CONTAINER

A wooden salad bowl, 30cm (12in) across and 15cm (6in) deep, is used here, but a shallow wicker bread basket is an ideal alternative, especially since wicker is similar to old-fashioned gardening baskets and trugs. If you use a glass bowl, buy extra moss to line the sides to hide the florist's foam block. A large kitchen mixing bowl would be ideal, as would an old copper or brass preserving pan, as long as it is not too deep.

A wide container is necessary to let light and air reach the lower foliage to keep it looking healthy. A wide, flat base will prevent the container from being knocked over in a busy kitchen. The container should be waterproof; if not it should be lined with plastic. It should be deep enough to allow room for watering and to allow the root-balls to grow freely.

CHOOSING THE SETTING

The featured display is photographed on an old-fashioned, wooden draining board, but in reality, few people have room on their draining board for anything other than newly washed dishes, pots and pans.

If you have a large kitchen table, then use the arrangement as a centrepiece. This display would look beautiful where it can be enjoyed by all the family at mealtimes.

If you are expecting guests, you can easily transfer the arrangement to a coffee table, but move it back when the guests have gone.

LOOKING AFTER THE DISPLAY

A kitchen can get very hot, especially when you are cooking. The display will last longer if you can move it at night to somewhere cool, such as a hallway or cloakroom. To avoid a build up of ethylene, which can shorten the life of cut flowers, ensure there is some ventilation in the kitchen, but don't put the display next to an open window. Avoid placing the arrangement near ripe fruit and vegetables as they also exude ethylene vapours.

REVITALISING YOUR DISPLAY

Regularly water and spray-mist the flowers and foliage, especially when temperatures are high. As soon as they wilt, remove cut flowers and foliage from the arrangement and add replacements. Once the polyanthus stop flowering, plant them outside, in the open ground, or in a tub or window box in a slightly shaded spot.

If there is a dramatic difference between the temperature inside and

This fragrant *pot-et-fleur* features cut stems of lilac, narcissus, pink anenomes and euonymus, tucked between pots of red polyanthus and miniature roses

out, wait for a while, otherwise it can shock the plants. The miniature ivy can also be planted outside, or you can use it as the starting point for a completely new *pot-et-fleur*. An alternative way of creating a *pot-et-fleur* is to plant a variety of pot plants in a bowl of earth and then add cut flowers to the growing display. First, line the bowl with broken crocks for drainage mixed with some charcoal to keep the compost 'sweet', then add a layer of potting compost. Remove the plants from their pots carefully and arrange them in the bowl. Fix the plants in position with more compost and water. Sink a small glass or foam-filled plastic container in the soil and arrange your chosen cut flowers.

COUNTRY
CASCADE

Fresh and dried flowers and foliage are not generally combined in the same display as the colours of fresh flowers tend to emphasize the muted shades of the dried ones, especially if the same type of flower is used. In addition, dried flower stems, especially herbaceous perennial ones, are difficult to dry again properly once they have become wet. They may rot and become useless for future displays.

This project overcomes both of these obstacles. The dried material used is hakea foliage. It looks so unusual that fresh material won't overshadow it. The stems are bound with waterproof gutta-percha tape before being inserted in the saturated foundation, so the stems will remain dry and can be used again.

The display is front facing and built up in a wire-mesh hanging basket, lined with polythene and fitted with a florist's foam block. It is relatively large, but can be scaled up or down according to your needs.

CHOOSING THE FLOWERS
The featured colour scheme is green, purple and peach. Flowers of virtually any colour can be used, though it works best if you stick to a background framework of lush greenery.

Bells of Ireland, or shell flower, is better known in its dried form than fresh. Its tiny flowers are hidden by green, bell-like calyxes, densely packed on a long flower spike. You can use the green seed pods of annual

mallow instead, or blue, white or pink larkspur, or even the green, unripe seed pods of wild polygonum.

Lady's mantle (*Alchemilla mollis*) gives double value for money. After it has been used in its fresh form, it can be dried and enjoyed again. Ideally, flowers should be dried just before they reach their prime.

Single daisy chrysanthemums from

As delightful as a country walk, this hanging basket is overflowing with fresh chrysanthemums, ornamental alliums, lady's mantle and ivy, with dried hakea foliage

the florist come in an enormous range of colours, any of which would be suitable. For a more dramatic impact, you could use the large daisy faces of pastel coloured single-flowered gerberas. Shasta daisies, pyrethrums, single dahlias or roses, cosmos, wild daisies or chamomile scattered in the display, would create a casual effect. Such garden flowers would look lovely hanging from the ceiling of a family sitting room.

Like chrysanthemums, florist's single carnations are available in many colours. Our display features peach carnations to match the same delicate shade in the chrysanthemums.

Trachelium, or throatwort, may need to be ordered in advance. The stalks in the display have been stripped of their long-stemmed side shoots. The mature purple and immature green flowers are then inserted separately, giving the effect of two completely different flowers.

UNUSUAL FLOWERS

Ornamental alliums are hardy bulbous plants, related to onions and leeks. Garden varieties range from miniatures, only a few centimetres high, to the enormous *Allium giganteum*, that can be as wide as 15cm (6in), with densely packed pink flowerheads carried on 1.5m (5ft) high stems. You will probably have to order them in advance. Alternatively, use mop-head hydrangeas.

CHOOSING THE FOLIAGE

Trailing green and white variegated ivy and arching stems of emerald feather asparagus fern are shown. Galax could be substituted, or golden-variegated or plain-leaved ivy. Whatever you use, make sure you buy enough to provide a dense waterfall of greenery.

Another idea is to take a *pot-et-fleur* approach. Buy some small potted ivies, ferns or even tradescantias. Remove the pots to make the root-balls more malleable, place them in the hanging basket, and gently feed the long stems through the wires.

Hakea is a tender evergreen shrub of the protea family, and is sometimes sold as Victoria protea. Its huge, wavy-edged leaves set it apart from the other foliage as much as its glaucous grey colour and dried texture.

CHOOSING THE FOUNDATION

A wire frame hanging basket has been used for this project. These are sold in garden centres, and come in various sizes, and in plastic-coated green, white and black as well as plain. There are also half baskets, for fixing to a wall. If you compose the display in a half basket, protect walls by lining the back of the basket with plastic.

The basket will hold a standard-sized saturated foam block. Make a plastic lining to prevent water dripping on the floor by cutting down a thick, plastic shopping bag or dustbin liner.

1 2 stems of bells of Ireland 2 3 hakea heads 3 5 stems of lady's mantle 4 bunch of peach single chrysanthemums 5 4 allium heads 6 8 stems of trachelium 7 6 peach single carnations 8 6-8 lengths of trailing ivy 9 10 lengths of asparagus fern 10 wire hanging basket 11 florist's foam block 12 scissors 13 sheet of plastic

PUTTING TOGETHER
YOUR HANGING BASKET DISPLAY

1 Hang the basket from a hook so that you can work easily. Line it with a sheet of plastic. Immerse a block of florist's foam in water and place it inside the basket. Bind the ends of three hakea heads with gutta-percha tape. Insert the stems through the plastic and into the foam, one angled down towards the right and the other two on either side at right angles.

2 Cut the ends of six to eight trails of green or variegated ivy to gradated lengths up to 1m (3ft) long. Insert into the sides of the basket and into the foam through the plastic sheet. The ivy stems should be strong enough to pierce the plastic itself, but if not use the sharp end of a knitting needle. Position the ivy trails evenly around the basket.

3 Remove the thorns from about ten trails of asparagus fern for easier handling. Ease the ends through the sides of the basket. Insert some sprays into the top of the foam for a full feathery effect. Trim two bells of Ireland stems. Place them vertically in the foam to set the height of the display, one slightly to the right-hand side, the other to the left.

4 Cut the ends of five stems of lady's mantle at a slant. Place one stem each side of the foam, angled downwards, and three in the centre of the foam, angled upwards. Trim eight trachelium stems to about 45cm (18in), removing any tall side shoots. Position the trachelium evenly throughout the display. Add the tall side shoots to add extra height.

5 Divide four chrysanthemum stems into florets. Insert deep into the foam block to give depth and to fill any gaps. Make sure that none of the foam is visible. Trim the stems of six carnations, leaving some almost full length and others about 30cm (12in) in length. Place one long stem to the right and one to the left of the arrangement. Position the others in a staggered line.

6 Trim four allium heads to different lengths, between 45-60cm (1½-2ft) long. Place one stem vertically just under the wire that holds the basket. Add the others randomly to the front of the arrangement. Check that there are no gaps showing foam and hang the basket in its final location. Spray-mist the flowers occasionally to prolong their freshness.

SEASONAL
SPLENDOUR

The dense, richly textured crown of this dried-flower tree is made entirely of natural and artificial berries, nuts, cones and pods. Leaves only play a minor role, as decorative cover to the container. The tree would look equally at home in a modern setting as in a traditional one and is particularly suitable for display in a cosy study or hallway.

This all-round display features a section of slender natural tree trunk, held upright in quick-drying cement. The surface of the cement is hidden by a layer of sphagnum moss; moss is also used to fill the globe-shaped chicken-wire foundation that supports the pods, nuts, cones and berries.

This is an ambitious project, not in terms of difficulty but in size and quantity of materials; however, you could scale the tree down to make a miniature version or a series of trees, in smaller leaf-covered containers.

The colour scheme is a typically autumnal one, with the browns and russets of the natural pods and cones enhanced by the bright orange, red and blue hues of the artificial berries. The larger pods, nuts and cones are used individually, while the smaller items are wired into tight clusters of a single type, for greater impact.

For a dramatic winter tree, you could select the different ingredients just for their interesting textures and spray them with white gloss paint, using car aerosol paint spray. Then, for a festive, Christmas touch, you could spray the tree lightly with gold, copper or bronze metallic paint. Alternatively, cover it lightly with synthetic snow.

APPROPRIATE MATERIALS

The proportions of the different materials used do not matter, as long as the end result is an interesting variation in both size and texture. Go to greengrocers, street markets or large supermarkets for the nuts; and to florists for the other ingredients. As an optional extra, give all the ingredients a light spray of clear polyurethane varnish to bring out their rich tones. Allow the varnish to dry completely before you begin to work.

Nutmeg is better known in its powdered form, but whole nutmegs are also available from grocers and delicatessens. Pecan nuts have a similar shape and smooth surface, and are also less expensive; you could use them or walnuts, which have a rougher texture, as a substitute for the whole nutmegs.

Chestnuts are cheaper still and, like the nutmegs, are wired individually. In the autumn you could gather your own horse chestnuts, or 'conkers'. For extra textural interest, try using them with their prickly cases intact.

Larch cones are not available commercially, so probably you will have to gather them from the wild. Alternatively, you could substitute other small conifer cones, such as pine or cryptomeria; some florists stock ready-wired pine cones. Otherwise, use twice the quantity of small proteas, which are similar in size and shape to larch. If you can't get these, use burdock seedheads or wired-up acorns.

Poppy seedheads are available in many sizes; choose fairly small ones, in natural silver grey. Alternatively, use small carthamus heads instead; their orange fluffy centres would suit this colour scheme perfectly. Love-in-a-mist seed pods or small lotus seed pods are other options.

Cedar cone bases are what remain after the cone falls away. You may have to order these specially from your florist. Wired-up, small dried fungi or beech mast could be substituted instead.

ARTIFICIAL BERRIES & PODS

Artificial berries and pods are available from home-decorating or haberdashery sections of larger department stores, large garden centres, craft shops and florists. It doesn't matter which berries you choose as long as they are small, glossy and bright.

Blue-black colouring is provided by artificial blackberries and ivy berries, wired into tight clusters. Deep blue bilberries, or blueberries, provide a lovely contrasting white sheen, as do the crimson imitation cranberries, also wired into clusters.

Artificial miniature pumpkins, perfect in every detail, look highly effective. In addition, they provide the excuse for displaying real pumpkins alongside as accessories.

Use real and artificial cones, pods and berries to make an unusual ever-lasting tree that's beautifully autumnal

CHOOSING THE TRUNK

A section of tree trunk, 60cm (24in) long, is used for the tree stem. If you live in the country, finding a suitable piece of wood should be easy. Otherwise, try to find out when trees are pruned in public parks and go and collect a few pieces before they are taken away. If necessary, use a length of bamboo curtain rail, a thick wooden dowel, or even a sturdy, hollow card-board tube camouflaged with bamboo, cane or bark.

Never rip branches from trees; the ragged wounds are likely to become infected. Also, for the sake of your secateurs, always use a small saw on branches or trunks that are over 2.5cm (1in) in diameter.

CHOOSING THE CONTAINER

An inexpensive, round wicker basket, 25cm (10in) high and 20cm (8in) wide, is used here, but it is hidden completely by its covering of overlap-ping rows of glycerined magnolia leaves (see box on page 90 for instruc-tions on how to decorate a container).

You could use almost any container, from an empty tin to a glass jar, glue-ing the leaves with strong, transparent adhesive instead of wiring them. Make sure, however, that none of the

DECORATING THE BASE

To camouflage the container, trim the stem ends from at least 24 glycerined magnolia leaves. Take six of the smaller leaves and place them one at a time horizontally against the bottom of the basket, so that they overlap each other. If necessary, use more leaves to encircle the basket completely. Fasten each leaf in place with a stub wire bent into a hairpin shape and pushed through the weave of the basket. Cover the sides with larger leaves, pinned side by side so that the tips point upwards. Make a second layer of smaller leaves, again placed vertically on top of the first layer. Tie a skein of twine around the covered basket to hold the leaves in place and provide an extra decorative feature.

1 24 glycerined magnolia leaves **2** 24 clusters of artificial blackberries **3** 24 clusters of artificial ivy berries **4** 2 bunches of nutmegs **5** 9 artificial miniature pumpkins **6** 2 bunches of chestnuts **7** 4 bunches of larch cones **8** 2 bunches of poppy seedheads **9** 2 bunches of mini protea **10** 24 clusters of artificial red berries **11** 24 clusters of artificial frosted bilberries **12** 10 cedar cone bases **13** handful of moss **14** wires **15** chicken wire **16** secateurs **17** tree base, quick-drying cement, string, hammer, nails

metal or glass shows on the inside of the rim. If necessary, use extra leaves or a thick layer of sphagnum moss to hide an unsightly container.

GLYCERINED LEAVES

Glycerined evergreen magnolia leaves (*Magnolia grandiflora*) are shown here, but you can use glycerined elaeagnus, beech, Solomon's seal or oak leaves, for a rich chestnut colour. To repeat the very dark, almost black look of the glycerined magnolia foliage, use glycerined mahonia, sweet chestnut or Lenten rose (*Helleborus orientalis*) leaves. Dried

leaves are unsuitable, as they are fragile and shatter easily.

If you cannot get glycerined leaves, use the wicker basket as it is or apply quick-drying glue to the basket and cover it with moss. Add the pretty natural twine bow, for a finishing touch. Alternatively, wrap the container in chamois leather or fake 'suede', in rich, natural tones, again fastening it with twine and splaying out the top to form a decorative, frilly edge.

CHOOSING THE SETTING

The featured autumnal setting provides display ideas that can be re-

interpreted on a more practical level. You could scatter a few attractive leaves round the base of the display, or position a little pile of nuts, or a dish filled with nuts, complete with nut crackers, nearby. A wooden salad bowl filled with glossy conkers makes an inexpensive prop. Alternatively, fill a dish with colourful ornamental gourds, or even a group of small pumpkins for a Hallowe'en-inspired display.

This arrangement is tall in relation to its width, and should fit comfortably on a narrow hall table, or corner or end table.

SIMPLE STEPS
TO MAKING A SEASONAL NUT AND POD TREE

1 Cut a narrow tree trunk to a length of 60cm (24in). Cut one end to a point. Stand the blunt end in a pot of cement until hard. Place the pot inside a basket. Hammer three or four nails a short way into the top of the trunk. Roll a clump of moss in a piece of chicken wire, to form a ball shape. Push the ball on top of the trunk. Cover the cement base with moss.

2 Separate four bunches of larch cones, attached to sticks. Cut to a length of 10cm (4in). Bunch them together in groups of three and place them evenly over the moss base. Wire the clusters of artificial blackberries to create false stems. Insert one cluster alongside each cluster of larch cones. Press the wire stems firmly into the moss.

3 Cut the wire stems of the mini protea to a length of 10cm (4in). Position one or two alongside each group of larch cones and artificial blackberries. Break off the small stalk from the middle of each cedar base. Insert one alongside each group. Add one nutmeg to each group. The smooth surface of the nutmeg provides a contrasting texture.

4 Cut the ready-wired chestnuts to a length of 10cm (4in). Group them in threes and introduce them into the base beside each cluster of materials. Cut the stems of the ready-wired, artificial miniature pumpkins and position alongside the chestnuts. The groups of nuts and berries begin to blend, creating an even rounded covering of richly textured material.

5 Wire together clusters of four or five artificial frosted bilberries. Cut the wired stems to a length of 10cm (4in). Open out the clusters of berries and use them to fill in the gaps between each group. Wire together four or five poppy seedheads and, again, cut the stems to a length of 10cm (4in). Incorporate them into the design.

6 Wire the red berries into small clusters. Spray some with leafshine to give them a gloss finish; leave the others frosted. Position them all over the moss base, filling in every space so that it is covered completely. Make sure that the finished tree has an even, rounded shape. If necessary, insert a few more wired chestnuts for greater variation of texture.

FRUITS OF
THE FOREST

Late summertime yields a wealth of very interesting flower arranging material. Ornamental berries are at their best, and many fruiting crops, such as blackberries, plums, apples, crab apples and pears, also are in their prime and make handsome additions to fresh flower arrangements. This all-round, informal display uses this seasonal bounty to the full.

The arrangement is inexpensive and simple to construct in relation to its size and impact, due to the high proportion of foliage. Even if you have

Combine florist's flowers, fresh leaves and berries from the garden and hedgerow with artificial fruits for this bountiful display

to rely entirely on florist's foliage for your requirements, the cost should still be comparatively low.

The colour scheme is typical of late summer, with the hot reds, russets and yellows of the flowers and the rich purples of the fruits, and cooling green foliage.

CHOOSING THE FLOWERS

If you have a garden and the first frost hasn't yet come, pick your own dahlias, early chrysanthemums and asters and use these instead of the flowers we have chosen. Otherwise, all the blooms featured in our display should be available from florists.

Yellow lilies provide large, trumpet-shaped blooms which contrast with the other, round-headed flowers. You can use orange lilies or yellow or orange alstroemeria instead, but avoid the pink or white varieties as these would lessen the impact of the late-summer colour scheme.

Yellow and bronze double spray chrysanthemums are typical late summer blooms. Single, spider or spoon-petalled spray chrysanthemums in rich colours would suit this display, but white daisy chrysanthemums would look too summery. Some florists offer mixed bunches in the yellow, orange and russet range, which make a pleasant alternative. If you choose to substitute alstroemerias for the lilies, try to use large, florist's chrysanthemums instead of spray varieties, to provide the necessary contrast in scale.

Red and yellow helichrysums, or strawflowers, may still be available fresh at this time of year. They are cheap and double value for money, since you can air dry them afterwards, provided they are not over-ripe.

Red spray carnations are available all year round and their colour helps add to the seasonal feel of the design. Rich orange spray carnations can be substituted, but may have to be ordered in advance.

CHOOSING THE FRUITS & BERRIES

A good mix of fruits and berries is more important than any one type; when selecting material, aim for variation in scale, texture and colour.

Long stems of blackberry, or bramble, and flat heads of elderberry add a touch of the wild. Neither is particularly welcome in the garden, but both grow profusely in hedgerows and waste ground. You can buy stems of blackberry and elderberry from some top-class florists, but they are very expensive, since they are not grown or distributed commercially.

ARTIFICIAL FRUIT

The real blackberries are supplemented with plastic blackberries, an optional extra that can be omitted without spoiling the effect. Plastic plums also are used; they have an attractive, natural-looking appearance. Larger florists, garden centres, and interior decoration sections of department stores often sell artificial fruit.

Artificial grapes or pears could be substituted, but avoid fruits with a summery feel, such as peaches and strawberries. Buy top-quality artificial fruit, even if it means buying fewer items; they can be used time and time again and you can always add to your collection later. Most artificial fruit is sold on short stems, but you can wire them up easily, for added length, and hide the wire amongst the foliage or cover it with gutta-percha tape.

Branches of fresh crab apples or small apples would be a lovely alternative to artificial fruit, but branches of huge Bramleys would be out of scale.

CHOOSING THE FOLIAGE

Normally, raspberry canes are cut down in late summer and you can cut as much as you like without harming the plants. If you have a local pick-your-own farm, ask if you can have a few canes. By late summer, weather and insect damage mean that raspberry foliage often is less than perfect, but this adds to the country-style charm of the arrangement. Black-

PRESERVING THE BERRIES

Berries are used in this display to give it a touch of the 'mellow fruitfulness' of late summer. However, once they are brought into a centrally heated room, they lose moisture quickly and may shrivel and drop.

Combat this by conditioning the berried plant stems before arranging them. Cut the ends at an angle and stand them in warm water for several hours. After conditioning, but before arranging, spray the berries with an even coat of hair spray. Protect surfaces by standing the stems in an upturned cardboard box.

To give the berries a glossy shine as well as preserving them, try spraying them with polyurethane varnish (available from craft shops). Apply a second coat if necessary.

could be used, but avoid highly decorated containers – even a glimpse of a pattern would detract from the informality of the flowers and foliage.

CHOOSING THE SETTING

This is an ideal transitional arrangement for a hall or porch, since it combines elements of the garden and hedgerows with highly cultivated florist's material. It forms a unifying link between the waywardness of the uncultivated outdoors and indoor stylized displays.

Make sure the display is positioned where it cannot catch on clothes or skin; blackberry and raspberry canes have thorns that can inflict a nasty scratch. If you use real blackberries and elderberries, keep the display well away from precious linen, damask and lace. Berry juice can leave a stain on fabrics that may be impossible to get rid of, and is hard enough to remove from laminated surfaces.

LOOKING AFTER THE DISPLAY

Keep the florist's foam topped up with water. Spray-mist the display regularly to keep it looking fresh and remove the faded blooms and any wilted foliage. When dismantling the display, cut off the waterlogged section of the helichrysum stems and hang them upside-down in small bunches to dry. These can be kept for use in permanent dried-flower arrangements.

berry, tayberry or sunberry foliage can be used instead. They are not normally sold by florists, but purple or copper beech would also be ideal, or you could substitute laurustinus or beech foliage if nothing else comparable is available.

Cotoneaster horizontalis is used here for its tiny leaves and the growth habit that gives it the common name, fishbone cotoneaster. Its large-leaved relatives would fit comfortably in the display and could be used instead, as could arching sprays of broom, or sprays of florist's galax or ivy.

CHOOSING THE CONTAINER

A round, rope-coiled wicker basket, 15cm (6in) high and 23cm (9in) across, is used; its natural colour, with shades of brown, russet and beige, emphasises the seasonal theme. A wood-bark or mossy basket would also be suitable, but avoid ones with handles, which would interfere with the construction of the display. Oval or square baskets of similar proportions would give a similar effect.

As the basket is partly hidden and therefore not a key feature in the display, a simple white china container

MAKING A
SEASONAL FLOWER AND FRUIT DISPLAY

1 Wedge a quarter of a block of soaked florist's foam into the bottom of the polythene-lined basket. Put a second piece on top with 1cm (½in) protruding above the rim. Trim four or five raspberry stems and three or four stems of cotoneaster foliage to about twice the height of the basket. Begin to cover the foam, placing the foliage so it appears to radiate from the centre.

2 Add the elderberry stems and the real blackberries for greater variety of texture and colour. To reproduce the feeling of natural woodland, you will need three or four leafy stems of each. Trim the stems to about 15cm (6in) long. Thin out some of the leaves from the bottom of the stems, remove any dead foliage and position the stems at random throughout the basket.

3 Use five lilies and two bunches of chrysanthemums to add colour. Trim the stems to12cm (5in) long and remove the lower leaves. Arrange some in a ring around the outer edge of the basket, then work towards the centre. Sit some flowers deep into the foam to give depth to the design. Save the best lily spray until last and place it in the very centre for maximum impact.

4 Cut two bunches of the red and yellow fresh helichrysum flowers and one bunch of red spray carnations so all the stems are 12cm (5in) long. Position them throughout the display so the red blooms are evenly distributed. Make sure the silhouette of the display is not too uniform. When the display is over, dry the fresh helichrysums for future arrangements.

5 Wire three plastic plums and six plastic blackberries on 25cm (10in) medium-gauge stub wires. Attach the wires near the end of the artificial stem so the wire will be hidden in the foliage. Cover with gutta-percha tape if necessary. The stems of the plastic fruits are fairly short, so make a long enough artificial stem to allow the tiny fruits to be clearly visible.

6 Bend the wired plastic plums and blackberries into natural-looking shapes. Position one plum stem at the front of the basket and one each side at the back. Place the six blackberry stems throughout the arrangement. Turn the display to check that all the florist's foam is covered and that the plant material is evenly distributed.

SAY IT WITH FLOWERS

Flowers have always been a favourite token of affection, and gifts especially made by the giver are equally highly prized. There are many delightful and unusual ways of combining the two and 'saying it with flowers'

In this chapter we look at flowers from a rather different point of view. Instead of concentrating on ways of making decorative displays, we have turned our attention to some of the many and varied items which can be made with flowers, for use in and around the home, and to give away as presents.

The scented gifts range from floral hand cream, scented bath oils and bath sachets to perfumed candles decorated with pressed flowers. Making your own hand creams and bath oils means that you know for certain that they contain only pure natural ingredients. However, home-made creams, which do not contain all the preservatives used in shop-bought products, do not last so long and should not be kept for more than a few weeks.

There's also the perenially popular pot pourri, redolent of the charm of life in comfortable country houses, and advice on how create your own blends. Pot pourris have a magical quality and yet they are surprisingly easy to make.

Dried flowers are used to decorate a straw boater, and to make a bouquet which is placed in a glass-covered frame to hang on a wall. Foliage, flowers and seedheads are also used to make a sumptous frame for a mirror or a picture. Then, for those with patience, there's a pressed flower picture which is reminiscent of a nineteenth-century sampler.

Naturally, there's a wide choice of edible gifts, both sweet and savoury. Choose between a delectable conserve made with red rose petals and a flower butter flavoured with apples and honeysuckle, or crystallise violets and other small spring flowers and

use them to decorate chocolates, cakes or biscuits. Oils and vinegars can be flavoured with sweet petals or with herbs. Not only do they capture a fleeting taste of summer, they're simple to make and if you choose elegant jars and bottles, they make a most attractive kitchen decoration.

However, one word of warning, before experimenting with floral flavourings, first read our Guide to Edible Flowers on page 119.

Wrap your gifts in suitable floral style. Make pretty tags and labels with a drawing of the relevant flower or herb, and use floral patterned wrapping paper or boxes.

Flowers in many guises. *Opposite,* a straw boater with a circlet of dried flowers. *Left,* a dried flower bouquet in a glass-covered frame, and (*right*), a nourishing hand cream made with marigold petals

SUMMER SPICES

A decorative bowl filled with pot pourri makes an evocative and natural alternative to aerosol room fresheners and is kinder to the ozone layer. Although you can buy pot pourri mixtures ready-made, making your own is easy and rewarding. All you need to do is stir together your chosen ingredients.

There are many recipes for pot pourri available and, once you have mastered the basic principles of blending flowers and spices for aroma, colour and texture, you will find it is not necessary to follow a recipe precisely. There is plenty of scope for modification, adding and substituting ingredients to create your own mixture. Simply keep a record of any changes you make so that you can recreate your successes and avoid reproducing any disappointing pot pourri blends.

The overall appearance of pot pourri is every bit as important as its aroma, so always select some ingredients for their visual appeal and others for their fragrance. Also, consider the colour and the design of the container to be used and where it is to be displayed before you start making your pot pourri.

CHOOSING THE INGREDIENTS

Richly perfumed flowers make up the bulk of any pot pourri, and sweet scented roses in particular are a popular ingredient both for their attractive petals and their delightful fragrance. Other appropriate fragrant flowers include lavender, pinks, sweet peas, jasmine, orange blossom, honeysuckle, and hyacinths.

Dried fragrant flowers are not always attractive looking, so include some unscented flowers in your pot pourri to lend shape and colour. Try using a selection of pansies, marigolds, forsythia, cornflowers, nasturtiums, delphiniums, forget-me-nots, borage, everlasting flowers and larkspur to achieve a pleasing look.

HERBS AND SPICES

The primary reason for including herbs and spices in a pot pourri is to add fragrance. The most commonly used herbs are bay, lemon balm, lemon thyme, rose geranium, rosemary and peppermint. Popular pot pourri spices include cardamom, coriander, nutmeg, cloves, cinnamon, allspice, mace, root ginger, anise and vanilla pods.

If possible, dry your own herbs or buy ones that have been dried recently. Likewise, buy new spices every time you make pot pourri and always buy them whole to grind or crush yourself. Try to be circumspect when adding spices as their fragrance should complement and add subtle nuances to the main fragrance rather than dominate it.

Occasionally, whole cloves, cardamom and coriander seeds, allspice berries, pieces of cinnamon stick or ginger root also are added to the pot pourri to provide additional visual interest.

Bring the heady atmosphere of high summer to cold winter days with this exotic pot pourri blend of flowers, herbs and eastern spices

CITRUS PEEL

Dried citrus peel adds a fresh aromatic contrast to the essentially sweet perfume of the flowers. Oranges and lemons are used most often, particularly in traditional recipes, but you also can use the peel from limes, grapefruit and soft citrus fruits. Pot pourri often includes essential oil to boost or complement the main fragrance. Essential oils are highly concentrated so add them in very small quantities.

A vital ingredient in any pot pourri is a fixative to blend the component fragrances and to retard the evaporation of the flowers' essential oils, thereby preserving their scent. The most commonly used fixative is orris root, usually in powdered dried form. Orris root comes from the rhizome of a member of the iris family and has a violet scent that contributes to the overall mélange of perfumes. Gum benzoin, which comes from a tree native to the Far East, is also a popular fixative; others include myrrh, frankincense and patchouli. Fixatives are available from herbalists and some chemists.

Once you have mixed the ingredients together, you will have to be

DRYING CITRUS FRUIT PEEL

Cirtus peel can be dried easily at home. But, as it takes up to a week to dry, the peel must be prepared well in advance.

1 You will need the rind of one or two oranges and lemons for this pot pourri. Use thin-skinned fruit if possible. Cut the skin off in large pieces. Scrape any excess pith off the skin. If the pith is left on, the fruit skins will not dry properly and the citrus smell will be impaired. An effective way of removing the fruit skins without the pith is to use a potato peeler.

2 Place the peel on a tray covered with kitchen paper and put this in an airing cupboard to dry. Alternatively, dry the peel in a oven on a very low heat. Keep the prepared peel in a lidded jar until needed.

1

2
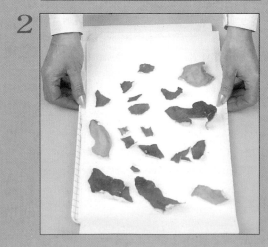

1 285ml (½pt) of dried helichrysum flowerheads 2 2-3 tbsp of juniper berries 3 570ml (1pt) of dried lavender 4 450ml (¾pt) of dried rose petals 5 450ml (¾pt) of dried rosebuds 6 150ml (¼pt) of dried bay leaves 7 150ml (¼pt) of dried thyme 8 150ml (¼pt) of dried rosemary 9 2 tbsp of both dried orange and lemon peel 10 2 whole nutmegs 11 2 cinnamon sticks 12 2-3 small pieces of root ginger 13 1 tbsp anise 14 1 tbsp whole cloves 15 1 tbsp coriander seeds 16 pestle and mortar 17 2 tbsp orris root 18 tablespoon 19 teaspoon 20 chopping board 21 knife 22 lidded jar 23 2-3 drops of rose oil 24 measuring jug

patient and wait for about six weeks to allow the various scents to mature and blend with each other and give the pot pourri a rich, evocative fragrance.

CHOOSING THE CONTAINER

The traditional perforated pot pourri pot is still a charming way to display pot pourri but they are not easy to find these days. However, there are plenty of alternative containers, such as rose bowls and sugar bowls. Large open bowls look superb filled with pot pourri, and this doesn't have to be as expensive as it sounds. Cheat, by packing the bowl with cotton wool or tissue paper and covering just the very top with a layer of pot pourri.

MAKING
SPICY SUMMER POT POURRI

1 Buy dried rose petals and buds or dry your own fresh roses. Carefully remove the good petals and place them on a tray lined with kitchen paper. The petals can overlap slightly. Repeat this process with whole rosebuds. Put the tray in an airing cupboard for about a week until the petals have dried completely. Expect some shrinkage in petal size.

2 Break up the helichrysum flowerheads into individual petals until you have the equivalent by volume of 285ml (½pt) of petals. Keep some of the smaller, prettier flowerheads to one side to decorate the finished pot pourri mixture. Measure 570ml (1pt) by volume of lavender. Add to the bowl and, using your hands, carefully mix with the helichrysum petals.

3 Measure 450ml (¾pt) by volume of both rosebuds and dried rose petals. Combine these with the helichrysum and lavender mixture. Roughly break up the equivalent by volume of 150ml (¼pt) of bay leaves. Avoid making the bay leaves too small as the overall look of the pot pourri will be powdery. Mix the bay leaves with the other ingredients by hand.

4 Add 150ml (¼pt) by volume of both rosemary and thyme to the pot pourri. Next, add the juniper berries. These are not fragrant but add variation to the pot pourri texture. Cut, break or grind the dried orange and lemon peel into small, uneven pieces (see box opposite). Add two tablespoons of both orange and lemon peel to the pot pourri mixture.

5 Next, add the spices. Roughly grind the whole cloves, coriander and anise with a pestle and mortar. Add one tablespoon of each to the mixture. Break the cinnamon stick into uneven pieces and chop the root ginger. Slice the nutmeg into thin slivers. Mix thoroughly with the other ingredients. The spices will give the pot pourri its distinctive aroma.

6 Shake two tablespoons of powdered orris root into the mixture to act as a fixing agent and mix in thoroughly. Lastly, add two to three drops of rose oil to the pot pourri. Again, blend thoroughly. Place the pot pourri in a lidded jar and leave for six weeks. Shake the mixture every other day until it has matured. Display, adding any flowerheads you have kept to one side.

PERFUMED
FLORAL CANDLES

Candles are surprisingly easy to make at home, and once you have grasped the basic principles you can go on to create more individual versions. In no time at all, you'll find that you are making candles to burn and work their magic all over the house – in the hall, living rooms, bedrooms and even in the bathroom. The colour of your candles, and the type of dried flowers used to decorate them, can be chosen to tie in with the colour scheme of the room in which they will be used. The floral perfume could reflect the season, such as lilac in spring, or the occasion on which the candle is to be burnt, musk rose, for example, would be the ideal choice for a romantic meal.

THE MAIN INGREDIENTS

The main ingredient used in making candles is paraffin wax. This can be bought at craft shops or department stores in either easy-to-use granules, or in blocks, which have to be broken up into smaller pieces with a hammer. 500g (1lb) of wax will make several good-sized candles.

Stearin (stearic acid), which is also widely available, is the second main ingredient added to the wax. It makes the candles harder, burn for slightly longer, makes them easier to release from the moulds by causing the wax to shrink slightly and minimises the drips. Use one part stearin to nine parts wax. Add too little stearin and the result will be a soapy candle; too much, a brittle one.

THE WICK

Care should be taken when buying a length of wick for your candles. Wicks are available in a number of sizes; the greater the intended diameter of the candle, the thicker the wick you will need. Cut your wick to the required candle length by measuring it against the side of the mould. A wick that is too small for a candle will not burn evenly and a shell of unburnt wax will build up and eventually extinguish the flame. If a wick is too large, on the other hand, the flame is likely to be very smoky.

CANDLE MOULDS

Flexible candle moulds can be bought in a wide range of shapes and sizes. It is also possible to improvise at home. Suitable containers must be able to withstand the temperature of the hot wax (test your mould with hot water before starting on the candlemaking operation), and must have a small hole in the centre of the bottom – either pierced or drilled through the base – for the wick to pass through. Fruit juice and milk cartons and some types of plastic yoghurt and cream cartons all make very good improvised moulds.

To make coloured candles, simply

The gentle glow of candlelight is comforting and relaxing. Add the perfume and decoration of flowers and the combination is irresistible

DECORATING CANDLES WITH PRESSED FLOWERS

1

2

1 To level the bottom of the candle, rub it around a warm, empty saucepan or slice it away with a sharp knife. To decorate your candles, position the flowers and leaf material on the candle in your desired pattern and attach them with transparent glue.

2 Next, dip your candle quickly in and out of a warm saucepan of wax (without added stearin), holding it by the wick. This seals the flowers in the right position. Leave in a warm, dry place for several days to harden. Finally, cut the wick to the required length.

add one of the candlemaking dyes
that are specially designed for the purpose; 1g of dye will colour 500g of
white wax. Dyes for colouring candles
can be bought as sticks, discs or, occasionally, as a powder or liquid. Wax
dyes are concentrated so add them
carefully – it is easy to add a little
more, quite impossible to remove any.
Sprinkle or pour the dye into the melted stearin so that it is completely dissolved before adding it to the wax. A
combination of colours can be added
for greater variety or to make more
subtle shades.

MULTI-COLOURED CANDLES

To create a straightforward multicoloured, layered appearance, pour a
small amount of different coloured
waxes into the candle mould, one at a
time, allowing each layer to set completely before adding the next one. To
give the layers an attractive 'twist',
carefully lay the mould slightly on its
side so that the wax sets on a slant. In
this way, each layer can be set at a different angle.

FRAGRANT CANDLES

To perfume your candles, use fragrant
dried flowers or, if these are not available or their scent requires a boost,

WAX WATCH POINTS

• Never leave wax unattended over
heat as it is highly inflammable.
• If you spill hot wax on yourself,
don't wipe it off, but run cold water
over it immediately so that it
solidifies.
• Remove the wax from the heat
when it reaches 32°C (90°F). If the
wax gets too hot, the finished candle
will have pit marks caused by
bubbles of steam on the surface.

1 2 saucepans (one larger than the other) 2 bucket or bowl of cold water 3 thermometer
4 500g (1lb) white paraffin wax 5 100g (4oz) stearin 6 wick rod pack 7 candle mould
8 transparent glue 9 blue tacky clay (mould sealer) 10 small paintbrush
11 wooden spoon 12 wooden stick to secure wick 13 pressed flowers and foliage,
candle dye pack (optional), and essential floral oil (optional).

then add a few drops of essential floral
oil. This should be added to the wax
just before it is poured into the mould.
Specially treated essential oils are
available specifically for candlemaking, but ordinary essential oil can also
be used.

DECORATING WITH DRIED FLOWERS

Give your finished candles a personal
finishing touch by decorating them

with pressed flowers and foliage.
Arrange them carefully on the surface
of the candle. Use a pair of tweezers
or the end of the paintbrush to pick up
the flowers and a small paintbrush to
dab on clear glue. Alternatively, you
can try sealing your flowers in place
by pressing them into position with
the back of heated spoon. To give
your candles a truly professional finish, polish them with a soft cloth and a
drop of cooking oil.

MAKING FRAGRANT
PRESSED FLOWER CANDLES

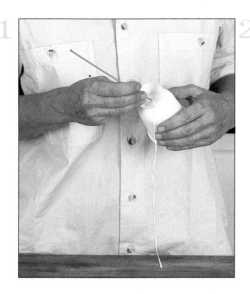

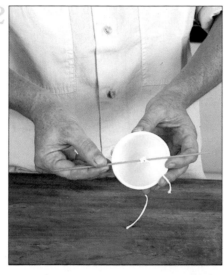

1 Make sure the mould is clean. Cut a length of wick at least 15cm (6in) longer than the mould. Make a hole in the bottom of your mould (if it is home-made) and using a wooden stick poke your wick through the hole, leaving a long end. Seal the hole underneath the mould with blue tacky clay.

2 Now use the wooden stick to secure the wick. Lay the stick across the top of the mould and wind the wick around it to hold it in place. The wick should be tied loosely; do not tie it so firmly that it bends in the middle. Leave the mould in a warm place while preparing the wax. This improves the finish of the candle.

3 Fill the large pan with water and place it over the heat. Place 500g of paraffin wax (this amount will make about six candles) in the smaller saucepan and insert it in the larger pan to melt. Keep the pans on a low heat.

4 As it melts, test the temperature of the wax with the thermometer. Check the level of the water in the larger pan from time to time and top up when necessary. Do not leave wax once it is on the heat. Add the stearin (and dye if required) to the saucepan as the wax is melting. Add essential oils now if you are making scented candles.

5 Remove the wax from the heat when it reaches 32°C (90°F). Do not allow it to get any hotter. Carefully pour the wax into the mould, making sure that it is held at an angle (other-wise air bubbles will form in the wax), and keep the wick dead centre.

6 Once it is full, place the mould in a bowl of cold water to cool down the wax so that it sets hard. Place your mould in the fridge to speed up the process. Your candles should be ready in an hour. Once set, remove the blue tacky clay and slide the candle out of the mould. If the candle sticks, run the mould under hot water.

PRESSED FLOWER
SAMPLER

A pressed flower picture can reflect any mood, colour or season. It can be as original and individual as its creator and designed from a wide range of materials.

Our featured display takes advantage of the delicate flowers of spring, arranged in a formal, linear design, reminiscent of an old piece of needlework. We use soft, glowing colours like the hues of faded embroidery threads, but you could choose to make up a rich, vibrant design of blues, reds and purples or design a pressed flower tapestry in subdued colours and soft textures.

Samplers were used originally to demonstrate a variety of stitches in the days before printed pattern books became available in the early sixteenth century. Later, in the seventeenth century, they changed their function and became a school exercise for young girls. Many charming examples survive from the eighteenth and nineteenth centuries.

CHOOSING THE FLOWERS

Suit your design to match the season, the pressed flowers you have available and the range of colours and textures you want to feature. You can either buy pressed flowers or press your own. To press small flat flowers, such as pansies, cut off unwanted stalks and foliage and flatten the flowers gently with your fingertips. Arrange them on a piece of blotting paper, making sure they do not overlap. Gently separate any overlapping petals so they lie as flat as possible. Fold over the blotting paper and place it in a flower-press and put it in a warm, dry place. Pressing bulky flowers like carnations is a little more difficult. Slice the bloom in half, then snip off the leaves and press these and the two half flowers separately. Never press thin and bulky materials on the same sheet. Flat flowers can be ready in four weeks, bulky flowers take somewhat longer.

The featured sampler uses delicate spring flowers and foliage in natural tones – tawny hawthorn and elderflower, mellow gold broom, narcissus, primrose and alyssum, creamy cow parsley, snowdrops and spiraea, crisp white daisies and arabis, olive green ivy and clematis set off by violet aubrieta, blue forget-me-nots and russet wallflowers.

The mauve heather border resembles running stitch and the border of sweet cicely looks like feather stitch set with tiny black heads – just like an embroidered sampler. The structure reflects a spring garden with its mixture of cultivated and free-growing flowers and foliage. Cow parsley springs up through a hawthorn hedge, while grass and moss grow among primroses and self-sown forget-me-nots. For interesting colours and textures, you could include ferns, seedheads, toadstools, lichens, bark, skeletonised leaves, rice and pulses, although these bulky ingredients will be difficult to fit into a glass-fronted frame. For a child's room you could use brightly coloured lentils to spell out the child's name, surrounded by a border of daisies.

CHOOSING THE BACKGROUND & FRAME

The background needs to be chosen as carefully as the flowers. Use stiff card as a firm base on which to mount the backing fabric. Avoid using very thick card or you may experience problems when it comes to fastening the frame. You could use a simple and cheap clip or snap frame, readily available from hardware and framing shops, or ask for the glass to be cut to your specific requirements, as in the featured display. Secondhand frames from markets and junk shops can make unusual and unique settings.

As a backing for the arrangement, we have used a neutral oatmeal-coloured Irish linen to offset the flowers. Use only natural fibre fabrics as synthetics show up the glue and often look too bright and gaudy. Undyed silk and cotton would be ideal for a neutral background, while brocade and velvet would suit a rich, vibrant composition.

The cream cotton lace is reminiscent of old tatting and provides an inner frame around the flower display.

Recapture the charm of an old-fashioned embroidered sampler with a simple arrangement of pressed spring flowers

Alternatively, you could edge a picture in embroidered ribbon, beaded or fringed trims and incorporate glitter, beads or tiny shells into the design.

COMPOSING YOUR DESIGN

This display takes a lot of time and patience to put together. If you can, try to allow yourself a full day to make the sampler, otherwise put it aside carefully to continue at a later stage but keep it covered with the glass from the frame. Pressed flowers absorb moisture from the atmosphere and may curl up if they are left exposed for any length of time.

PREPARING A BACKING

Cut a piece of stiff backing card to fit the size of your snap-frame backing exactly. Cut a piece of your chosen backing fabric about 2.5cm (1in) larger than the card to allow for folding over the edge and iron flat. Centre the card on top of the fabric and brush a thin layer of glue around the edges of the material. Fold the edges over the card, leaving the corners unstuck. Press down firmly, keeping the fabric taut so there are no creases and making sure the weave of the material runs straight. Fold down the corner into a triangle then bring each side over to form a neat, mitred finish. Repeat for the other three corners.

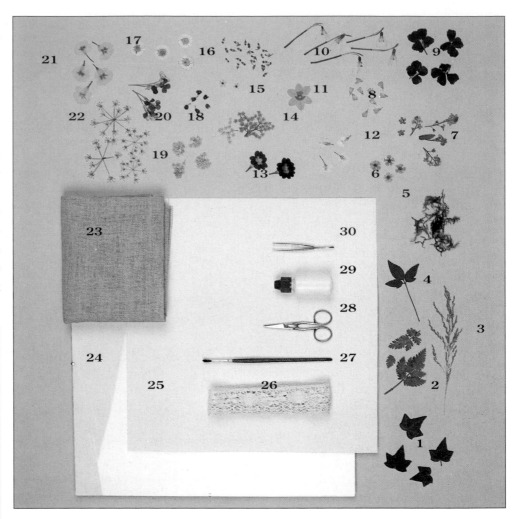

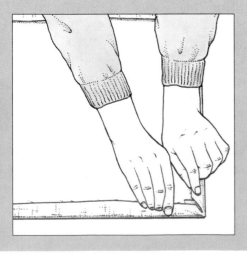

1 4 ivy leaves 2 1 stem of sweet cicely 3 1 stem of grass 4 2 clematis leaves 5 1 clump of sphagnum moss 6 12 hawthorn flowers 7 1 cluster of forget-me-nots 8 1 stem of broom 9 4 wallflowers 10 5 stems of snowdrops 11 1 narcissus flower 12 1 cluster of arabis 13 2 primula 'Wanda' 14 1 cluster of elderflowers 15 2 *Spiraea thumbergii* 16 160 individual heather flowers 17 4 field daisies 18 1 stem of grape hyacinth 19 1 stem of *Alyssum saxatile* 20 2 clusters of aubrieta 21 6 yellow primroses 22 3 clusters of cow parsley 23 50cm (19in) square of beige Irish linen 24 35cm (14in) glass snap frame 25 1 piece of firm card 26 1m (39in) length of cream cotton lace 27 small brush 28 small scissors 29 latex-based glue 30 tweezers

Lay your materials on a piece of paper and experiment with the composition before beginning your arrangement on the fabric. If the design is very complicated, make a sketch first. Make sure that it is balanced in proportion and colour, always keeping in mind an idea of its final size.

Have your materials easily accessible on a clean, dry surface. Brush or blow away dust particles as you work. To avoid damaging the delicate pressed material, pick up each flower with tweezers and use a soft paintbrush to move them around. Use a latex-based glue rather than transparent adhesive as it does not leave a shiny finish. Use a tiny quantity on the end of a brush, applying it to stems or the bases of the flowerheads to avoid staining the petals.

When you have finished your design, stand it upright and tap it gently so any loose fragments fall off rather than becoming trapped under the glass and spoiling the design.

ASSEMBLING A SAMPLER
OF PRESSED FLOWERS

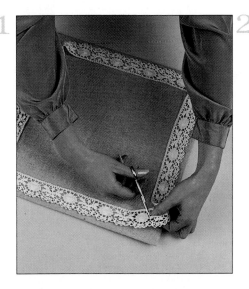

1 Lay the lace around the outside of the fabric-backed card (see box) 1cm (⅓in) from the edge. Cut the top right corner diagonally, in line with the corner of the backing. Cut the adjacent piece of lace diagonally to overlap the first piece, adjusting the pattern to match. Cut the other sides. Apply glue sparingly to the underside of the lace: press down firmly in position.

2 Place some glue in a saucer – a little at a time as it dries quickly. Trim the stalks off the heather. Hold each flower in the tweezers and lightly dab them into the glue. Place the flowers on the fabric, closely fitting them together, end to end, to form a border running parallel to the lace frame. Use the paintbrush to sweep away any tiny pieces of debris.

3 Put an ivy leaf in each corner, overlapping the heather border. Cut the clusters of cow parsley into pieces and arrange in trios between five hawthorn flowers, running down the vertical sides. With the end of a paintbrush, dab a minute blob of glue on each flower where the stalk meets the flowerhead. Slide the wallflowers under the tips of the ivy leaf and glue in place.

4 Glue and place small pieces of sweet cicely along the vertical edges. Put six broom flowers along the top left edge and six on the right. Between them, position two clematis leaves, with three arabis flowers below them. Place a cluster of forget-me-nots and an arabis flower on each side above the clematis and cover the stem ends with the narcissus. Glue to the fabric.

5 Glue three forget-me-nots and a triangle of grape hyacinth flowers on each side below the broom. Put a daisy in each corner. Make a horizontal line of spiraea, elderflowers and hawthorn, with a forget-me-not in the middle. Put a cluster of cow parsley inside the sweet cicely borders. Put a group of alyssum and a primrose on each side and a primula in the middle.

6 Place the snowdrops all together. Trim the grass and put it on either side of the snowdrops, with a primrose and cluster of aubrieta on each side. Flank the arrangement with two clusters of forget-me-nots and leaves. Snip the moss into pieces and glue onto the stalk bases. Put the sampler onto the frame base, place the glass on top and clip into place.

FLORAL FLAVOURS

Take advantage of fragrant fresh flowers to make edible treats for your friends and for your own larder. You don't need to be a great cook to create these delicious flavours, since no cooking is necessary. Simply impregnate standard kitchen ingredients – oil, vinegar, butter and sugar are suitable subjects – with the perfume of flowers, such as marigolds, elderflowers, violets, honeysuckle, lavender, roses, jasmine, clove pinks, freesias, orange or flowering herbs.

CHOOSING THE FLOWERS

Only use fragrant flowers that you know are edible. (See page 119 for a list of edible blooms.) Never use flowers that have been sprayed with insecticides or fungicides, nor ones which have been growing close to a road where they will absorb dangerous toxic fumes.

To gain the most fragrance, pick your flowers early in the morning or during the cool part of a sunny day, either just before they are in full bloom or at the height of bloom. They must be quite dry before use. Before you start, discard any damaged petals and shake off any insects.

Small flowers, such as chives, violets and lavender, can be used whole with just the stamens and green calyx at the base of the flowers removed. Use only the petals from larger flowers, such as clove pinks, marigolds and roses.

Attractive bottles of flower flavoured vinegars and oils add zest to marinades and salad dressings; they also make delightful gifts or decorations for a kitchen shelf

FLAVOURED VINEGARS & OILS

Add zest to wine vinegar and olive oil by infusing them with a handful of chive flowers, or other sweet petals, or with culinary herbs such as tarragon or basil. Use only wine vinegar because the strong taste of malt vinegar overwhelms delicate floral flavours. Choose mild, pure olive oil or a flavourless vegetable oil – and use the scented oil for frying as well as for salad dressings. Autumn salads dressed with these infusions will smell and taste of summer flowers.

Bottles and jars of oils and vinegars containing flowers and herbs displayed along a windowsill, either during or after preserving, also make practical and very attractive kitchen decorations.

FLOWER HONEY

Transform an inexpensive blended, but mild-flavoured honey into a luxurious preserve for spreading on bread, toast, scones and fancy tea breads; stirring into porridge and milk puddings; accompanying pancakes or waffles; and for using in cake and biscuit mixtures. Rose petals, orange blossom or scented geranium leaves can all be used.

Melt 450g (1lb) of honey in a bowl placed over a saucepan of hot water, stirring occasionally with a wooden spoon. Lightly bruise one cup of fragrant flower petals or leaves, then add to the honey and continue to warm gently for half an hour. Remove from the heat, cover and leave in a warm place for a week, giving the mixture an occasional stir. Place the bowl of honey over a saucepan of hot water again and reheat gently. Strain through a muslin-lined sieve into clean jars. Cover, label and keep in a cool place for a few days before using or giving away as a present.

FLOWER SUGAR

Use flavoured sugar when baking cakes and puddings; in sweet sauces; sprinkled on raw and cooked fruits; to

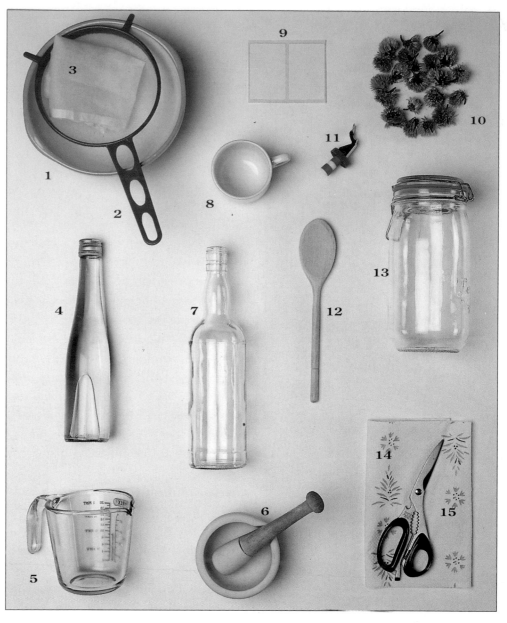

1 bowl **2** sieve **3** muslin **4** 600ml (1pt) white wine vinegar **5** measuring jug **6** pestle and mortar **7** glass bottle **8** cup **9** paper labels **10** a handful of chive flowers **11** airtight stopper **12** spoon **13** airtight jar **14** kitchen paper towels **15** scissors

DECORATING LABELS

Floral flavoured honey, butter, sugar, vinegar and oil make charming gifts to give to family and friends. Transform a simple jar into a special present for any occasion by decorating your labels with drawings of the appropriate flower or by attaching pressed flowers to them. To add to the recipient's interest in the contents, write clearly on the labels details of the ingredients, the date the gift was made and its storage life.

To continue the floral theme, wrap the gift with paper printed with flowers. Alternatively, adorn the wrapping paper or container with sweet-scented fresh or dried flowers tied around the neck or tuck a flower into the packaging ribbon.

flavour cream, fromage frais, soft cheeses; to serve with puddings or scones; sandwich cakes and biscuits together – on almost every occasion when you normally use plain un-flavoured sugar.

Mix two packed cups of flowers or petals with one cup of sugar for a strongly flavoured sugar or equal quantities for a mild one. Grind together using a pestle and mortar until the mixture is very fine. Spread on a baking tray lined with foil and leave for two hours in the warming drawer or a cool oven until the sugar has absorbed the moisture from the flowers and is completely dry. Leave until cold then pack loosely into clean jars and close with an airtight lid. Label and keep in a cool, dark place. A quick way of making scented sugar for short term storage is to bury dry petals or flowers in a jar of sugar. Petals from a highly scented dark red rose are a good choice, and dried rosebuds look exquisite buried in a jar of sugar.

MAKING
CHIVE FLAVOURED VINEGAR

1 Gather the chive flowers when they are at their most fragrant. Shake to dislodge insects and wash the flowerheads gently with a light sprinkling of clean water and toss them on kitchen paper to dry. Allow about 75ml (5tbs) of fresh flowers to each 330ml (½pt) of white wine vinegar. Snip off any blemished stalks or damaged petals with sharp scissors.

2 Lightly bruise the prepared chive flowerheads using a clean, dry pestle and mortar or by pressing them firmly with the back of a spoon. This helps release the fragrant oils from the petals and brings out the flavour, allowing it to impregnate the vinegar. Thyme, nasturtiums and marigolds are alternatives for flavouring culinary vinegar or oil.

3 Place the bruised chive flowerheads in a clean, dry, wide-necked jar. Measure the white wine vinegar into a jug and pour it slowly over the herb flowerheads. Close the lid of the airtight jar and make sure it is sealed securely against leakage when the jar is being shaken vigorously, or evaporation when it is standing in the sunlight.

4 Shake the jar to mix the flowers thoroughly with the vinegar. Leave the jar on a warm, preferably sunny, windowsill for several weeks. Shake the jar briefly every day so the oils from the chive flowers blend into the vinegar. Taste the vinegar regularly to see if it has reached the required flavour and strength. If not, leave it on the windowsill until it is ready.

5 When the vinegar is ready, place the sieve over the bowl. Drape the muslin over the sieve, ensuring that it covers both the sieve and the bowl so that any stray drips are caught. Slowly strain the scented vinegar into the bowl. (When preparing flavoured oil, take care to empty the jar completely.) Carefully lift the muslin off the sieve and discard the saturated flowerheads.

6 The vinegar may take on a coral pink tinge when it is maturing. Place a few fresh chive flowerheads in a clean bottle and pour the scented flower vinegar over them. Seal the bottle with an airtight and acid-proof stopper, label and store in a cool place. To sample them at their best, consume flavoured oils and vinegars within three months.

FLOWER
PRESERVES

The delicious flavours and scents of flowers can be sealed into an enormous range of jams and jellies, curds, butters (thick spreads with a high proportion of fruit) and cheeses (fruit preserves so thick that they can be potted in moulds and turned out to make attractive displays on the table). Spread rose-petal jam, elderflower and gooseberry curd, lavender jelly and orange blossom butter on tea breads, scones, sandwiches, crumpets and muffins. They can be used to fill cakes and pastries and stirred into puddings. Mix them with cream, fromage frais or thick Greek yoghurt to make a simple dessert, as a topping for summer fruit or to fill pancakes or tartlet cases. Conserves are delicious spooned over ice cream, while jellies enhance meat dishes.

Flower preserves can be made at home quite easily and, if made in bulk, will cost you a lot less than their commercial counterparts. Home-made flower conserves make charming and practical gifts, and look especially attractive if you cover the lids with floral fabric and design your own decorative labels for the jars.

SELECTING FLOWERS
Choose full-scented, edible flowers, such as fragrant roses, elderflowers, orange blossom, philadelphus, violets, lavender, clove pinks and honeysuckle. If you are picking them yourself, avoid blooms growing near roads, as there will have been some lead absorption, and flowers that have

The flower preserves, securely covered, can be stored with other jams and jellies in a kitchen cupboard. Keep them out of direct light to prolong their storage life

been sprayed with harmful insecticides or herbicides. Wash the flowerheads thoroughly to dislodge insects, and remove the stems and flower centres before use. Use the individual petals from flowers such as roses; elderflowers can be used whole. See page 119 for a complete list of edible flowers.

Flowers can be combined with sugar and water to make jams and jellies; mixed with butter, eggs and sugar to make curds, or blended with fruit. For example, rose petals blend very well with cherries; elderflowers with gooseberries or rhubarb; orange blossom with peaches or apricots; and honeysuckle with strawberries.

Always use the petals as soon as possible after detaching them from their stems as they will wilt very quickly and impair the flavour of the preserve. Add the flowers to the sugar mixture while it is cooking, either loose or tied in a muslin bag. Strain them for a smooth preserve such as curd, or leave them in, as in the rose-petal conserve featured in our step-by-step instructions.

PREPARING THE CONSERVE
Deep red, fragrant rose petals produce a distinctly flavoured conserve

POTTING CONSERVES

It is important to prepare all jam jars properly to preserve the contents and prevent your conserve from going mouldy. First, pour boiling water into the clean jars to sterilise them, or warm them in a preheated oven for a few minutes. Dry the jars thoroughly.

After spooning in the conserve, trim a waxed disc to fit snugly inside the neck of the jar. Wipe the rim of the jar with a hot, damp cloth. Cover the surface of the conserve with a disc, waxed side down. Press down to force out any air bubbles. This process hermetically seals the jar.

Finally, dampen one side of a cellophane jar cover with water and stretch it, damp side up, over the top of the jar and secure with a rubber band. The cellophane becomes taut as it dries.

FLOWER BUTTER

To make an apple and honeysuckle butter, simmer together 1kg (2lb) of cored and chopped eating apples, a cup of prepared honeysuckle flowers and 300ml (½pt) of water for 30mins until the apples are soft. Pass the mixture through a plastic sieve and weigh the pulp. Add 350g (12oz) of sugar to every 450g (1lb) of pulp. Slowly heat the mixture, stirring with a wooden spoon until the sugar is dissolved. Cook gently over a low heat, stirring frequently until the mixture has the consistency of thickly whipped cream. Spoon it into clean, warmed jars, cover and label.

1 10 bunches of fragrant roses 2 450g (1lb) granulated sugar 3 lemon squeezer 4 2 lemons 5 kitchen scales 6 2 glass jars 7 adhesive labels 8 2 cellophane jam lids 9 2 waxed discs 10 rubber bands 11 wooden spoon 12 metal spoon 13 saucepan 14 measuring jug

which is most delectable. First, the petals are covered with some of the sugar and left to stand overnight so the scent is drawn out and the colour darkens. The mixture is then simmered so that it is not as thick as a conventional jam or jelly. All preserves must be potted and sealed properly.

PROLONGED SHELF-LIFE
Store all preserves in a larder or other cool, dark place, with the exception of curds, which need to be kept in a refrigerator. Most preserves improve in flavour if left to mature for a few days after they have been made. They will keep for as long as a year if they are sealed and stored correctly; however, their flavour does deteriorate eventually with prolonged storage. Cheeses will improve over a period of a few months but curds should be eaten quickly and not stored for longer than a month.

MAKING
ROSE PETAL CONSERVE

1 Remove the fragrant rose flowerheads from the stems. Discard any blemished or bruised petals. Using your thumb and nail, pinch out the bitter white heels of the petals. Wash the petals thoroughly in clean water without detergent to remove dust and insects. Weigh the prepared petals to make sure you have 225g (8oz). Scatter them over kitchen paper or a clean towel to dry.

2 After weighing, place the rose petals in a large kitchen bowl. Weigh 225g (8oz) of the sugar and sprinkle it over the petals with a spoon, covering them thoroughly. Lightly stir in the sugar. Place a cover securely over the bowl and store it in a cool, dark place for 12 hours, or overnight, to allow the petals to darken to a deeper red and their sweet scent to be drawn out.

3 Slice two large ripe lemons in half and extract the juice. Strain and remove the pips and any loose pieces of skin, and skim any residue from the surface. Pour 1 litre (1¾pt) of fresh tap or mineral water into a large stainless steel saucepan. Do not use an enamel pot, as the red liquid may stain it. Add the lemon juice and stir it into the water.

4 Spoon in the remaining sugar. Heat the sugar, water and lemon juice mixture gently over a moderate heat, taking care not to bring it to the boil. Do not heat the sugar too rapidly otherwise it may caramelize. Stir it thoroughly with a wooden spoon until the liquid feels smooth and you are sure all the sugar has dissolved properly.

5 Empty the rose petals into the saucepan. Stir them into the sugar and water mixture, taking care not to break up the delicate petals. Heat the mixture gently until it simmers. Simmer without stirring for 40 minutes. Bring to the boil and boil steadily for about ten minutes to reduce the liquid and thicken the mixture. The conserve should have a syrupy consistency.

6 Skim any residue from the surface. Spoon the jam into warmed, sterilised jam jars. Cover with waxed discs, then dampened cellophane jam pot covers. Secure with rubber bands. When the jars have cooled, write the date, name of the conserve and use-by date on an adhesive label and fix it securely to the front of the jar. Store out of direct sunlight in a cool place.

FROSTED FLOWERS

Spring favourites such as primroses, cowslips, primulas and violets are perfect flowers for crystallising, not only because of their diminutive size and pretty faces, but also because they are not very robust and quickly wilt when picked.

Crystallising is a traditional method of preservation that is quick and easy and needs no specialised equipment or ingredients. It is the ideal way to create pretty, natural decorations to go on top of gifts of chocolates or other sweets, either home-made or shop-bought.

CHOOSING THE FLOWERS

First and foremost, only use flowers that you are certain are edible (see the box on the right for more details). Flowers that are flattish with a small number of petals, such as violets or primroses, are the easiest to use. Whatever time of year you are crystallising flowers, do not use any that have been treated with pesticides or fungicides or exposed to car exhaust fumes or other types of pollution. Select only perfect undamaged specimens with no bruises or brown marks.

There are many species of violets – the ones to choose for crystallising are the purple or white flowers of *Viola odorata* (sweet violet). This variety flowers in early spring and sometimes in autumn. The best time to pick flowers for crystallising is on a fine morning after the dew has lifted. This is when they are freshest and have the most fragrance and flavour.

The flowers must be clean and completely dry, otherwise the crystallising solution will not adhere properly, the flowers will discolour and they will not last long. If they need washing, a fine spray of water is all that is needed. Do not soak them completely. If they are slightly damp, lay them on some absorbent kitchen paper. If you are crystallising a complete flower, as opposed to petals, leave it on a small length of stem so that it is easier to handle. The stem can be trimmed after crystallising.

Capture the freshness of your favourite spring flowers beneath a sparkling coating of sugar and transform an ordinary box of chocolates into a personalised gift

GUIDE TO EDIBLE FLOWERS

Be very careful when choosing flowers to crystallise. If you are unsure about whether or not a particular flower is edible, always double check in a reliable reference book or with an expert. If you are in any doubt at all, then don't use it.

Make sure that you don't pick flowers that have been growing near a road or that might have been sprayed with insecticide. Always avoid using flowers that have grown from a bulb.

The following flowers are all edible and suitable for crystallising:

almond blossom – *Prunus dulcis*
apple blossom – *Malus sylvestris*
borage – *Borago officianalis*
carnation – *Dianthus caryophyllus*
clover – *Trifolium sp.*
cowslip – *Primula veris*
daisy – *Bellis perennis*
dandelion – *Taraxacum officinale*
elderflower – *Sambucus nigra*
forget-me-not – *Myosotis alpestris*
freesia – *Freesia x kewensis*
honeysuckle – *Lonicera periclymenum*
hydrangea – *Hydrangea macrophylla*
jasmine – *Jasminum officinale*
lavender – *Lavandula vera*
magnolia – *Magnolia grandiflora*
may blossom – *Crataegus monogyna*
mimosa – *Acacia dealbata*
nasturtium – *Tropaeolum majus*
orange blossom – *Citrus sinensis*
pansy – *Viola tricolour*
primrose – *Primula vulgaris*
rose – *Rosa gallica*

scented-leaf geranium – *pelargonium graveolens*
sweet william – *Dianthus barabatus*
violet – *Viola odorata*
yarrow – *Achillea millefolium*

Small and delicate flowers, such as freesias, primroses, forget-me-nots and individual rose petals, are all perfect for crystallising

DECORATING GIFTS

Crystallised flowers are a natural and attractive way to make many kinds of sweet 'edibles' look much more special. Use them to decorate Easter eggs, cakes, biscuits and desserts, whether you are serving them at home or giving them as presents. Crystallised flowers also make a gift in themselves, and will be doubly appreciated if packed into a pretty, airtight storage container.

A variety of decorative styles can be easily achieved without any particular artistic skill, simply by using different types of flowers or petals and varying the way in which they are arranged. For example, a single crystallised flower will give a fresh, bright 'clean' look, whilst a few flowers arranged together in a group and placed strategically add an air of elegance. Flowers that have been crystallised complete with their stems and leaves can also form a pretty design. And don't forget, you aren't restricted to using the leaves of the flower you are crystallising – small sprays of young mint or lemon balm make attractive and delicious alternatives.

THE INGREDIENTS

Crystallising flowers is a simple procedure. The first step is to apply a protective coating of either egg white or gum arabic. If egg white is used, the flowers will dry within an hour but they should not be stored for more than three days, whereas if they are sealed inside a coating of gum arabic you can keep them for some months.

Gum arabic is a colourless, flavourless, odourless substance, obtained from the acacia tree. It must be dissolved completely before use in either rose or orange flower water. Gum arabic and rose and orange flower water are available from chemists and also from some good grocers and super-markets. Whether you choose to use egg white or gum arabic, follow the same crystallising process.

To store unused crystallised flowers or petals, place them on layers of waxed or greaseproof paper in an airtight container. Put this in a safe dark place where there is no danger of it being accidently knocked or dropped.

DISPLAYING THE CHOCOLATES

The nicest way to display your chocolates is in a specially decorated box. Cardboard boxes in different shapes and sizes are available from most large stationery shops. Cover the box with some pretty paper or fabric and fill the inside with tissue paper or velvet in a matching colour. Decorate your container to suit both the occasion and the recipient. A heart-shaped box filled with decorated chocolates makes the ideal gift for Valentine's Day, chocolate eggs in a spring basket would be an unusual Easter present, or choose someone's favourite flowers to top chocolates for an extra-special Mothering Sunday treat.

To decorate a 450g (1lb) box of chocolates you will need:
1 15ml (1 tablespoon) gum arabic 2 3 x 15ml spoons (3 tablespoons) rose water or orange flower water 3 edible liquid food colouring (optional) 4 fresh, dry, perfect violet flowers or petals 5 caster sugar 6 selection of chocolates 7 chocolate for melting (milk or plain as required) 8 small saucepan 9 heat-resistant bowl 10 small screw-topped jar 11 small bowl 12 fine, soft paint brush 13 wire rack or tray lined with waxed or grease-proof paper 14 palette knife 15 spoon 16 scissors

CRYSTALLISING
VIOLETS IN SIX EASY STEPS

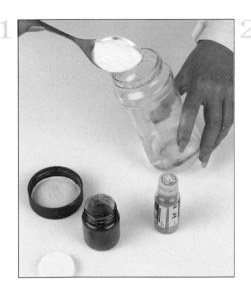

1 Dissolve 1 tbs of gum arabic in 3 tbs water. Add a drop of rose or orange flower water. For a more unusual look, or to add colour to white flowers, add edible food colouring. Put the solution in a screw-top jar and give it a good shake. Leave for three hours or until the gum arabic crystals have dissolved and the mixture has taken on a syrupy consistency.

2 Gently take apart a small bunch of violets. Select the best-looking flowers. Discard any that are damaged or dirty. Snip off the stalks just underneath the flowerhead. Make sure that each flower is completely dry. Place any damp flowers on absorbent kitchen paper.

3 Sieve the sugar if you require a very fine coating. Using a soft artist's brush, apply an even coating of the gum arabic mixture to all parts of each flowerhead. Alternatively, whisk a little egg white and use this to paint the flowerheads before coating with sugar. If you use egg white, the flowers will dry in one hour. Take care not to bruise the delicate petals.

4 Take a handful of caster sugar and sprinkle gently over the wet petals. If you prefer, hold each flowerhead with tweezers. Place the flowers on a wire rack or baking tray covered in greaseproof paper and leave to dry for at least 24 hours in an airing cupboard or other warm, dry place until they feel completely firm.

5 Once set, loosen the flowerheads from the greaseproof paper with a palette knife. The flowers are very brittle and will break easily at this stage. Handle them with great care to prevent damage to the flowers themselves or to their protective sugar coating.

6 Melt a small bar of dark or milk chocolate in a glass bowl over a pan of hot water. Keep stirring the chocolate. Put small blob of melted chocolate on top of each chocolate to be decorated. Quickly secure a single violet flower on the top of each chocolate. Finally, arrange the finished chocolates in a gift box.

HAT TRICKS

Flower-covered hats are among the most romantic images of spring and summer. Silk, polyester and mixed fibre flowers are often used to decorate hats, but you can also use dried flowers. Straw hats of any shape, colour or size are natural partners for dried flowers, since straw is simply dried stalks of grain.

When you are not wearing your straw hat, you can hang it decoratively on a wall, or decorate it extravagantly for more permanent display.

CHOOSING THE HAT

Straw hats can be tightly woven to form a rigid shape, such as this old-fashioned, flat-topped boater, or loosely woven and floppy. A rigid hat is a better choice for a dried-flower trim, since it forms a stable base and protects the delicate flowers from accidental knocks. You can also decorate a floppy hat with flowers, provided you always handle it carefully.

Choose natural straw, as shown, or a bleached ivory shade if you want a hat that goes with many colour schemes. Straw hats are also available in a range of dyed pastel and bold colours. However, these will limit the choice of flowers and clothes that can be teamed with them.

CHOOSING THE FLOWERS

For our straw boater, we used blue larkspur, white sea lavender, golden morrison (*Verticordia nitens*) and mixed colour helichrysums, or strawflowers. Most of these are inexpensive and widely available, although you may have to order the golden morrison in advance from your florist. Sea lavender is available in many dyed colours, though the natural white sea lavender shown gives the lightest and airiest effect.

The hat has a good balance of flower shapes and sizes, with the delicate sea lavender contrasting with the more solid forms of helichrysums, and the spiky sprigs of larkspur adding further interest. Almost any small or medium-sized dried flowers can be used; common sense is the best guide. Huge, dried globe artichokes or dried hydrangea heads would be unsuitable. However, a single large hydrangea head broken into florets and wired would provide plenty of attractive filler material to go round a hat brim.

For an alternative lacy filler, use cloud grass, *Agrostis nebulosa*, or gypsophila instead of sea lavender. Cloud grass, a hardy annual from Spain, produces little, loose clusters of hazy white flowers. Cloud grass is available in natural white and several dyed colours, but you will probably have to order it in advance. The thread-like stems are as delicate as the flowers, so wire them together into small bunches, using fine-gauge stub wire, before attaching them to the main wire encircling the brim.

A mixture of flowers and foliage is attractive, but dried leaves, such as dried rose leaves, are extremely brittle, and can shatter at the slightest touch. Glycerined foliage is more flexi-

Capture the charm of the countryside by decorating the brim of a favourite straw hat with dried flowers. It makes an unusual gift to wear or to display on a wall

ble, and is more likely to survive intact. Dark brown glycerined beech has autumnal overtones, but you could use golden, glycerined elaeagnus, or wine red, glycerined eucalyptus leaves instead.

CHOOSING THE RIBBON

Grosgrain is traditional hat ribbon, tough and long lasting. For a more glamorous effect, look through the haberdashery section of a large department store for ideas. Silk or polyester satin ribbon looks romantic, but it doesn't hold its shape when looped. Velvet may be too heavy and wintery-looking.

For an informal, country-style hat, you could plait strands of raffia into a suitable length to use instead of ribbon, or drape the brim with a softly-patterned silk scarf in colours to match the flowers. If you have made a dress to go with the hat, make the hat band and trailing ribbon from a length of extra dress fabric.

EASY ALTERNATIVES

The steps show wiring up a circlet of dried flowers for a hat. If you do not have time to create something so complex, but still want an attractively decorated straw hat, make a posy or clus-

1 1 bunch of helichrysum on cane stems
2 1 bunch of sea lavender 3 1 bunch of
golden morrison 4 1 bunch of blue larkspur 5 straw boater 6 gutta-percha tape
7 2 m (6ft) satin ribbon 8 floristry scissors
9 stub wires

dried flowers are more vulnerable to wet weather and accidental knocks than those decorated with silk or polyester flowers, so choose the occasions when you wear your hat carefully. If rain or windy weather threatens, or the venue is liable to be crowded, it is best not to risk damage to your hat. On the other hand, it would be perfect for a spring wedding, a picnic or a drinks party on a sunny day.

For an unusual effect, hang the decorated hat, a pair or even a trio of hats, on an entrance hall wall, or perhaps a living room or bedroom wall. Arrange the display at eye-level. Because the crown of the hat sticks out several centimetres from the wall, hang the hat above a piece of furniture, such as a table, to keep it safe.

As with any dried-flower display, bright direct sunlight will make the flowers and the colour of a dyed straw hat fade. A steamy atmosphere, such as a kitchen or bathroom, is also unsuitable, as the flowers and straw will rot.

LOOKING AFTER YOUR HAT

Even with the best care, some flowers will eventually become dislodged or disintegrate. If the damage is not too extensive, replace the damaged flowers with new ones. Carefully extract the broken ones, then work in the new stems with a short length of gutta-percha tape. If the damage is too great, remove the wire ring and start again. If you tire of the hat, carefully detach the main wire from the brim, then transfer the flowers to the brim of another straw hat.

DRIED FLOWER HAT CARE

• You should avoid wearing your hat in the rain, but this won't always be possible. Air-dried flowers, such as those used in our display, will eventually go mouldy if they are allowed to get wet. If you intend to wear your hat, it may be better to use glycerined flowers as they are more water-resistant.
• If your hat is likely to be knocked, spray it liberally with unscented hairspray to fix the flowers in position.
• When you are not wearing the hat, store it in a hat box lined with crumpled tissue paper.

ter of dried flowers and foliage instead. A quick trip to the hat department of a large department store will give you plenty of ideas.

Whatever flowers you use, make the posy front-facing and flat on one side, rather than all-round, since it has to lie flat against the hat. Backing a little posy with glycerined leaves makes a nice finishing touch. You can tack the flowers on the front, back or to one side of the hat or under the brim, close to the head.

CHOOSING THE SETTING

The most glorious setting of all is where a hat is intended to be – on the owner's head. Hats decorated with

DECORATING A STRAW BOATER
WITH DRIED FLOWERS AND SATIN RIBBON

1 If you cannot buy a long piece of wire, join several lengths of florist's stub wire. Overlap the ends of two wires by 2cm (1in) and twist together. Continue adding to the wire until you have enough to encircle the hat brim, less a 4cm (1½in) gap where you will secure the bow. Allow an extra 4cm (1½in) at each end to fasten the wire to the hat.

2 Cut two or three stems of sea lavender and larkspur about 2.5cm (1in) long. Lay the sea lavender on the wire, 4cm (1½in) from the end. Put the larkspur below the sea lavender. Wind a piece of gutta-percha tape tightly around the wire and stems and hold for a few seconds to bind the flowers. Wind the rest of the tape around the stems.

3 Select three stems of golden morrison and three helichrysum flower-heads, 2.5cm (1in) long. Use the golden morrison as a bushy background flower. Leave one helichrysum stem slightly longer and use this as the apex of a triangle made with the other two heads. Place on the wire overlapping the first floret to hide the wire. Bind as before.

4 Continue adding to the wire, using different flower combinations. Work on a flat surface to avoid inadvertently twisting the heads away from the lead flowers. If you find holding several heads at once cumbersome, try using smaller groups and build up slowly, or bind each flower group with tape separately and then attach the florets to the wire.

5 Keep adding flowers until you have just 4cm (1½in) of wire exposed at both ends. Trim any wild stems. Wrap the wire around the hat, making sure the flowers are facing outwards, and poke in both ends, leaving a 5cm (2in) gap at the back for the ribbon. Twist the wire inside the hat so that it is flush with the straw and tuck the sharp ends into the weave.

6 Cut two lengths of ribbon about 1m (3ft) long. Make two loops in the centre of one piece and secure with a piece of wire. Make two smaller loops in the second piece of ribbon. Hold these against the first loops and wrap the wire tightly around them. Thread the wire ends through the hat in the gap allowed and secure the ends. Trim the ribbon.

GOLDEN REFLECTIONS

A wooden mirror frame, extravagantly decorated with foliage and gold-painted dried flowers and seedheads, makes a magnificent focal point in any room. The gold and green hues used here will tone with most interior colour schemes but can be modified to match particular home furnishings by using different tinted spray paints.

You can decorate any wooden picture frame using this technique. If you have an old mirror frame that is beginning to look slightly worn, such treatment will give it a fresh lease of life. New wooden frames are available from picture framing shops and most specialist shops will make up a frame to your specifications, although this can be expensive.

In the featured design, two varieties of ivy – one with berries, the other without – are used to create a foliage base for the contrasting dried flowers and seedheads. Although the ivy appears fresh, in fact it has been preserved using glycerine. This method of preservation has the advantage of leaving plant material supple, an important consideration for this project as the foliage has to be manipulated to follow the line of the frame. If you prefer a flatter, copper-coloured foliage base, try using glycerined beech leaves.

SELECTING FLOWERS & SEEDHEADS

The dried flowers and seedheads have been chosen for their interesting shapes and textures; their colour is immaterial as it is obscured by the gold paint. Both the delicate Chinese lanterns and the poppy seedheads add a pleasing rounded detail to the frame decoration. Chinese lanterns tend to crumple if they are handled roughly or too frequently, even when they have a protective coating of spray paint, so they should be added to the frame after the other plant material has already been attached. As an alternative, use globe-shaped craspedia or physocarpus, which has dainty star-shaped seedheads. Poppy seedheads are more robust and the small crown at the top of the head gives added interest to their shape. Suitable alternatives include love-in-a-mist seed pods, echinops and small fir cones.

INTERESTING TEXTURES

The gold paint highlights the interesting textured surface of the golden mushrooms, but any other variety of dried fungi or seed pods could be used instead; for a particularly satisfactory alternative, try using dried lotus flower fruit which has an unusual pitted appearance.

Both carline thistles and wood roses have been selected for their attractive heads. Carline thistles make excellent feature flowers with their compact centres surrounded by a mass of spiky petals. Large protea flowers would be equally effective.

Carthamus tinctorius (dyer's saffron) and helichrysum flowerheads are used as smaller filler material. Carthamus flowers project from a cluster of pointed leaves; helichrysum heads are compact, spiky and round. Use both to fill in spaces between the larger feature flowers. Alternatively, if you cannot obtain these flowers, try using the elaborately petalled Jerusalem sage or hops.

Tiny wired berries and short lengths of twisted cane provide textural contrast. Any dried or plastic berries would be equally suitable, or you can use brunia which has a mass of small spheres on each stem. If your florist does not stock twisted cane, try making your own by soaking a short length of thin cane (available from craft shops) in water until it is supple and then coiling it around a pencil. Secure it with fine gauge stub wire and leave to dry over a period of two or three days.

USING A GLUE GUN

Although you can use ordinary strong adhesive to attach the plant material to the frame, it is unlikely to hold the weight of the plant material permanently. The cleanest and easiest method of fastening such a quantity of

Transform an old wooden mirror or picture frame with a lavish gold and green border of preserved foliage, flowers and seedheads

material securely is to use a glue gun. Available from hardware stores and DIY shops, glue guns plug into an electric socket to heat up. A stick of solid glue is inserted into the back of the gun and, as it melts, the glue is forced out of a nozzle at the front.

Once plugged into the mains, glue guns take between three and five minutes to warm up. The adhesive they use is quick drying and is strong enough to secure even the heavy trails of ivy used here. However, take care not to touch the glue as the adhesive becomes very hot.

There are two types of glue gun on the market: the basic model requires the operator to guide the glue stick through the gun with his or her thumb; a slightly more sophisticated version uses a trigger device to hold the glue stick in place. Although the triggered variety is marginally more expensive, it is much easier to operate

PAINTING THE FRAME

Cover your work surface with newspaper to protect it. Work in a well-ventilated room to avoid inhaling fumes. Clean the frame before applying paint so it goes on evenly. Shake the can of paint vigorously and spray the wood. You can cover the wood completely or spray it very lightly so that the attractive pattern of the wood grain is still visible.

1 1 small bunch of berried, glycerined ivy 2 1 bunch of 90cm (3ft) trails of glycerined ivy 3 half a bunch of Chinese lanterns 4 1 bunch of *Carthamus tinctorius* 5 half a bunch of poppy seedheads 6 8 golden mushrooms 7 1 bag of helichrysum heads 8 1 small bunch of wired berries 9 3 carline thistles 10 8 wood roses 11 5 short lengths of twisted cane 12 wooden frame, 75 x 60cm (30 x 24in) 13 gold decorative spray paint 14 scissors 15 polyurethane spray varnish 16 glue gun

as you can regulate the flow of glue. Buying a glue gun is a sensible move as it will prove invaluable for many dried flower projects.

FINDING A LOCATION

This elaborate frame is ideal for a hall. As the decorated frame would dominate any wall, it is best to display the finished mirror in a room which does not already have a natural focal point. Alternatively, the mirror would make a magnificent addition to any special celebration, especially a theme party.

To match a particular colour scheme, add a few choice dried flowers, such as roses, in a toning colour. The gold of the flowers and seedheads makes this display perfect for easy adaptation into a Christmas decoration. Simply add extra dried plant material spray-painted red and silver, or some festive bells and baubles.

Care for the frame by wiping the plant material from time to time with a damp cloth. Alternatively, you can blow off any dust using a hair drier on a cool setting.

DECORATING A FRAME
WITH IVY, FLOWERS & SEEDHEADS

1 Prepare the wooden frame (see box on page 128). Dust the dried flowers and seedheads well so that the spray paint adheres to their surfaces evenly; use a small, fine brush if necessary. Remove the Chinese lanterns, poppy seedheads and carthamus flowers from their stems. Snip off the stalks from the carline thistles and wood roses so that they will sit flat on the frame.

2 Place the flowers and seedheads on a piece of newspaper so that none of them touch. Shake the can of gold spray paint and, holding the can 25-30cm (10-12in) away from the plant material, spray the flowers, seedheads and twisted cane evenly. Leave to dry. If any plant material is to hang over the edge of the mirror, spray the undersides as well.

3 Working near an electricity socket so that you can use a glue gun safely, fasten trails of glycerined ivy to the frame with small patches of glue. Press the ivy stems firmly to the glue until they are secure – this takes about 30 seconds. Once the main stems are in position, glue the leaves into place. Add the berried ivy for contrast and to fill any gaps. Cover the whole frame.

4 Arrange the largest gold plant material – the carline thistles, wood roses and golden mushrooms – in a pleasing design around the frame. Using the glue gun, cover their undersides with glue and secure them to the ivy base. Press them firmly into place for about 30 seconds. Be careful not to allow your skin to come into contact with the adhesive as it is very hot.

5 Add the smaller plant material – the helichrysum, wired berries, poppy seedheads and carthamus – to the frame to fill in any gaps. Decorate the sides of the frame as well as the front. Incorporate the Chinese lanterns after the other plant material. Finally, add the short lengths of twisted cane, two lengths on the bottom of the frame and one on each side of the other sides.

6 Spray the ivy lightly with gold paint so that the foliage is linked visually with the gold flowers. If your frame already has a mirror or picture in it, make sure this is fully protected by a newspaper or a cloth held firmly in position. Leave to dry for about 10 minutes. Spray the decorated frame with a coating of polyurethane varnish for an attractive shine. Allow to dry.

PRETTY AS A PICTURE

A dried-flower picture is the perfect way to preserve much loved, home-dried garden flowers, or carefully chosen bought specimens from the florist. Very simple designs can be made to look extremely striking and dramatic against attractive backing paper and, once framed and covered in glass, dried flowers will retain their freshness and colour for many years to come.

BUILDING UP THE DESIGN

Unlike a pressed-flower picture in which every flower is stuck down, this design is held in place by the glass – the dried flowers are layered to form a posy effect and tied in place with a raffia bow. If the finished bunch is of the correct depth – neither too bulky nor too flat – it will be held securely in place by the glass front of the frame. A fine film of hairspray as a protective covering will strengthen dry, brittle stems and will prevent fragile flowerheads from dropping off when the picture is moved around.

To ensure that the design keeps its original shape and outline, avoid using dried material that disintegrates easily or flowers with thick heads such as daffodils or rosebuds. They will create too bulky a bunch and will be crushed against the glass.

COMBINING FLOWER SHAPES

Contrast of textures is all important when putting together your posy. Large, soft flowerheads form the focal point of a picture. We have used rose-heads, clematis and delphiniums but anemones, hydrangea florets and marigolds are possible alternatives.

Spiky plant material adds interest to an arrangement, especially to a posy display that is filled with smoother material. The tall spikes contrast with rounded blooms and with delicate, feathery material.

Coarse plant material provides the strongest three-dimensional effect and there is a wide variety of possible material in a range of colours and shapes. Choose from catkins and pussy willow, thistles and grasses and clumps of moss and lichens. Don't use too much coarse material, however, as the picture will look too heavy. You will need a selection of lighter, feathery plants for effective contrast.

The obvious choice for feathery plant material is dried gypsophila, but don't forget the equally delicate lady's mantle, asparagus fern, cow parsley and astilbe flower. They all soften the impact of colourful blooms and spiky or coarse material.

CREATING THE FIRST LAYER

To build up a layered bunch like the one we have featured you need a single, broad specimen for your bottom layer. We have used *Alchemilla mollis* for its natural fan shape but a fern leaf or a sprig of limonium, provided it is not too bulky, would both work just as well.

Long flower spikes of lavender and larkspur create the distinctive fan-shaped outline, but grasses, corn, oats, limonium or amaranthus can be used to similar effect. Gypsophila in its wide variety of dyed shades can be used as a filler instead of broom bloom, while daisies could well replace the open delphinium florets and fairy roseheads.

Display your dried flower bouquet in a glass-covered frame and create an original wall decoration

USING A FABRIC BACKING

Instead of using coloured paper as the backing for your dried-flower picture, experiment with different types of fabric. As a basic guideline, it is best to use natural fabrics rather than more brightly-coloured artificial materials, as the bright colours will clash with the muted shades of the dried flowers.

Silks, linens, cottons and even velvets all make suitable backings for a dried-flower picture. Choose unobtrusive neutral shades such as cream and beige if you want a more simple background. Textured fabrics such as lace or calico work best as backings for more vibrant designs.

Subtle shades of colour can be achieved by dyeing fabrics with dyes taken from natural plant materials. This results in backing shades that do not clash with the delicate plant material.

ADAPTING A FRAME

If your finished flower design is too bulky or your picture frame too shallow, you will need to add extra depth to it to prevent the plant material in the picture from being squashed against the glass. Cut thin strips of wood to length and stick them along the undersides of the four edges of the frame with a wood adhesive. This will build up an extra layer that lifts the glass away from the hardboard backing and so prevents the flowers from getting squashed. The glass should only press gently on the flowers.

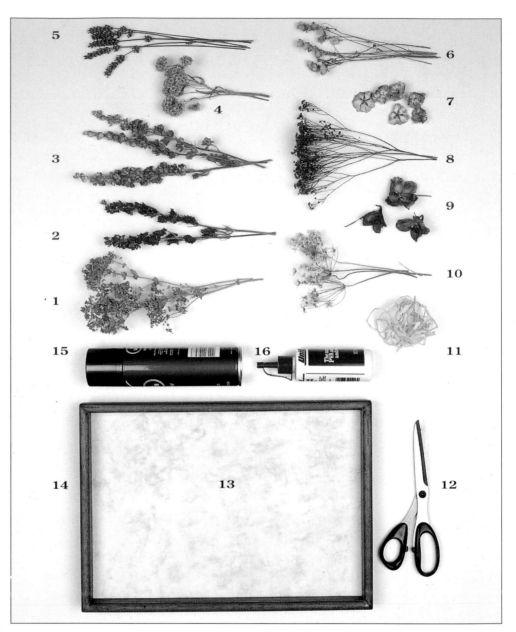

1 1 large, fan-shaped sprig of *Alchemilla mollis* 2 3 sprigs of mauve larkspur
3 2 sprigs of pink larkspur 4 3 sprigs of cluster-flowered helichrysum (*Helichrysum italicum*) 5 5 sprigs of lavender 6 1 small bunch of buttercups 7 6-8 small fairy roseheads
8 1 small bunch of Bordeaux-dyed broom bloom 9 2-3 blue delphinium flowers
10 3 sprigs of dill 11 30cm (12in) length of raffia 12 floristry scissors 13 backing paper
or card 14 oblong glass-fronted frame 2.5cm (1in) deep 15 hairspray
16 glue, small hammer, and tacks

CHOOSING THE BACKING PAPER

Experiment with a selection of backing papers in order to find one which both complements your choice of flower colour and provides a link with the frame. A white background can sometimes be too cold to set behind warm flower colours. A warmer shade is better but a marbled or flecked paper can be even more effective, especially if it picks out one of the flower colours. You will find a wide range of coloured and textured paper and card to choose from at any good art shop. The deep red of the broom bloom would provide a rich backing colour as well as blending in very subtly with the natural wood frame used. Alternatively, a pale warm grey or a canvas-coloured paper would create a lighter, brighter effect.

Cut the backing paper slightly shorter in length and narrower in width than the card backing you are using in order to ensure that the paper does not catch and crease when you come to fit the finished design into the glass-fronted frame.

FRAMING YOUR PICTURE

When choosing the frame for your dried-flower picture, remember that it must be 2.5cm (1in) in depth. If it is shallower than this the flowers will be crushed against the glass, and if it is deeper it will not serve its purpose of holding the bunch in place. You can

SIX STEPS
TO A DRIED-FLOWER PICTURE

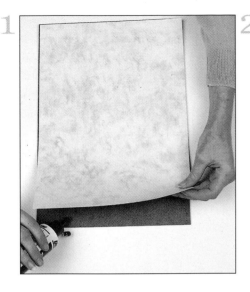

1 Put a sheet of coloured paper or card on the backing of the frame. Place it so that there is just a fraction of board showing along each edge. Taking care not to move the paper, lift the corners gently and glue in position. Instead of standard clear adhesive you could also use glue in a stick form. This is a drier glue and will not mark the backing paper or card.

2 Lightly spray each flower with an aerosol hairspray. This gives a fine protective cover and will prevent bits from dropping off as you arrange the bunch. Choose a large, fan-shaped piece of *Alchemilla mollis* and arrange it in the centre of the paper backing. There is no need to glue the flowers in place – just lay them in position on the card.

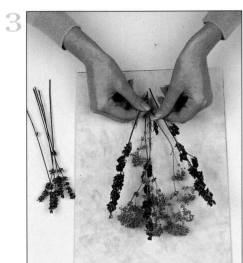

3 Fan out three stems of mauve larkspur in your hand – the longest in the middle and the two shorter stems on either side. Centre them vertically and use the two side stems to set the height of the design. Add two short sprigs of lavender to set the width at the base of the design and use the other three sprigs to build up the fan-shaped outline.

4 Form another layer with the three sprigs of *Helichrysum italicum*, arranged in a small crescent shape near the top of the bunch. Take the buttercups and spread them out across the front of the design with their heads just below the helichrysum florets. Arrange the two pink larkspur spikes at a slant to the left and right of the centre.

5 Carefully break off individual sprigs of broom bloom. Its small, delicate flowers make it an ideal filler to hide any gaps in the centre of the design. Insert the broom bloom among the flower stalks. Arrange the dill sprigs so that their fluffy white seedheads cover the bare stems of the other flowers and fill in any unsightly gaps in the design.

6 Take one of the open delphinium florets and place it in the centre of the bunch at the same height as the lowest dill seedheads. Place the other floret slightly higher to the right of the design. Insert one fairy rosehead above and one below the central delphinium floret. Scatter the others randomly among the flower stalks and at the top of the design.

have frames specially made to order at picture framing shops where you are able to specify the exact depth you require but this can prove a costly exercise.

Most picture or photo frames are shallower than the depth required for this dried flower bouquet but it is possible to adapt them by building up the depth of the frame with extra strips of wood (see box on page 132 for instructions).

Simple frames are nearly always the best choice for a display of this sort for an ornate, elaborate frame will overpower the delicate beauty of the flowers. It is important to make sure that the picture itself is always the most dominant feature.

Pine frames are fairly cheap and can often be found in secondhand and junk shops and at street markets. They provide a soft natural surround to most dried flower colours.

Alternatively, you can paint the frame in the colour of your choice. Spray paint gives a smooth, professional-looking finish and allows you the option of gold or silver tints as well as a wide range of other colours. For instructions on painting a frame, see the box on page 128.

MAKING AN OPEN-FRONTED FRAME

As a cheap and easy-to-make alternative, you can use the top of a rectangular cardboard shoe box as a frame. The cardboard will not be strong enough to support glass but you can use it as an open frame as long as the box is at least 2.5cm (1in) deep. Spray-paint the cardboard and cover the base with an attractive paper. Make up the dried-flower design directly into the frame and glue the base stems firmly to the backing paper. Finally, add a thick film of hairspray to hold the material in place.

FITTING THE DISPLAY
INTO THE FRAME

1 Once you have completed the bunch, pass a length of colourful raffia or ribbon underneath the stalks and secure the posy with an attractive single bow.

2 Make any final alterations to your finished display. Spray a thin film of hairspray over the whole bunch – this will hold the flowerheads in place and prevent any pieces breaking off.

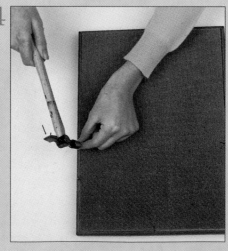

3 Place the card-backed floral design on a raised surface such as a book. Make sure the glass is clean and then place the frame carefully over the design. Use both hands to press the hardboard backing into the base of the frame. The glass of the frame should press down gently on the flowers.

4 Carefully turn the frame over. Using a small hammer, knock half the length of a small tack into the centre of one side of the frame. Knock the top end of the tack over towards the centre until it touches the hardboard backing. Repeat this using one tack for each side of the frame.

MARIGOLD
HAND CREAM

Home-made floral-scented hand cream is a natural and effective way to protect your hands and keep them soft, smooth and young looking. Combine your favourite flowers with a selection of natural ingredients for a rich and nourishing cream suitable for every type of skin.

Flowers play an important role in hand care, for as well as their sweet scent, they have special therapeutic properties. Marigolds, honeysuckle, roses and lavender all help to soothe, heal and soften rough hands.

A hand cream should keep skin smooth and supple by protecting it from moisture loss, preventing dirt from getting into the skin and restoring the balance of acidity that can be upset by harsh, alkaline soaps.

Our hands are constantly on view yet they are frequently taken for granted. Little attention is paid to keeping them in good condition and protecting them from the many forces that dry them out. Repeated exposure to sun, wind, cold, heat, dirt, water and household detergents all make hands rough and chapped. Often, it is not until an important occasion looms that we worry about the appearance of our hands, by which time it's too late.

REGULAR TREATMENT

The first step in basic hand care is to take simple preventative measures, such as avoiding direct contact with harsh detergents and household cleansers by wearing rubber gloves for washing up and gardening gloves

for gardening and similar rough tasks.

Home-made hand cream should never be sticky or greasy, but particularly dry skin does require treatment with richer creams. Older skin, especially, needs frequent moisturising as skin becomes drier and more sensitive with age.

NATURAL INGREDIENTS

Flowers can be used to make very simple preparations, such as floral rinses and infusions, but they are frequently teamed with other beneficial natural substances to make a wide range of effective beauty products.

Rich marigold hand cream will nourish and protect hands from the ill-effects of harsh detergents and household cleaners

Almond oil and ground almonds combat dryness and help to keep the skin lubricated and smooth. Honey can be used for healing cuts and sores, and glycerine and oatmeal for softening and moisturising. Oatmeal is especially useful, for as well as gently dislodging dirt, it is good for treating rough skin and acting as a skin healer. Lemon restores the natural acid bal-

1 fresh marigolds to make 45ml (3tbs) of petals 2 15ml (1tbs) of cocoa butter 3 15ml (1tbs) of white beeswax 4 muslin 5 screw-top pot 6 measuring jug 7 pestle and mortar 8 small, non-aluminium saucepan 9 sieve 10 2 heat-proof bowls 11 small bowl 12 small spoon 13 wooden spoon 14 tablespoon 15 small pinch of borax 16 few drops of rose oil 17 115ml (4fl oz) almond oil

when a water-based substance such as rose water is added, to blend all the ingredients together.

Beeswax, cocoa butter and borax can bought from good chemists, although they may have to be ordered specially.

STORING THE CREAM

Spooning home-made creams into small jars can be a difficult operation. Always use a small spoon and work a knife around the edge of the jar to remove air pockets. Some creams solidify after a few hours which makes them hard to get out of the container. Wide-necked jars are therefore a sensible choice. If you have stored your hand cream in a bottle, it may be too thick to get out at all. If so, warm the cream first on top of a radiator or in an airing cupboard.

Home-made hand care products do not keep as well as commercial ones that contain preservatives and stabilisers and should therefore be kept in a cool place, away from direct light. Home-made hand creams should be kept in screw-top, airtight jars. Those containing perishable ingredients, such as milk, should only be made in small quantities, stored in the refrigerator and used within a few weeks.

To prevent any traces of bacteria from getting into your home-made hand cream, always make sure your hands are perfectly clean before dipping them into the jar.

ance of the skin, upset by the alkalinity of many soaps, and, as it is a mild bleach, it removes stubborn dirt. If used in too concentrated a form, however, it will dry the skin. For everyday use dilute it with moisturising, softening ingredients. Vinegar, especially cider vinegar, works in the same way as lemon and it is also beneficial to the condition of the skin.

MAKING THE CREAM

White beeswax and cocoa butter, two natural ingredients, are often used in the making of home-made hand creams as they are good emollients and barrier creams. In most recipes they are mixed with an oil, such as rich, nourishing wheatgerm oil or

almond oil, as well as floral oils. The choice of floral oil rather than the flowers used will determine the scent of your finished hand cream.

The greater the proportion of beeswax to oil that is used, the harder the cream. About eight parts oil to one of beeswax produces a creamy consistency, but you can experiment with different proportions to reach a thickness that suits your needs. When using cocoa butter, do not melt it with the beeswax and oil, but beat it into the mixture after it has been removed from the heat. Borax, a white, crystalline mineral powder, is often included in recipes using beeswax and cocoa butter as it acts as an emulsifying agent. It is an important ingredient

SIX STEPS
TO MARIGOLD HAND CREAM

1 Pull the petals from about six fresh marigolds to make approximately three heaped tablespoonfuls. Discard the flower centres, leaves and stems. Crush the petals using a pestle and mortar or with the back of a wooden spoon. This releases the plant juices and prepares the petals for infusion in hot water.

2 Empty the crushed marigold petals into a small, heat-resistant bowl. Pour 160ml (5-6fl oz) of boiling water over the petals. Avoid using aluminium, copper and non-stick pans as their chemical contents can affect the natural ingredients adversely. Cover the bowl with a lid or plate and leave the liquid to cool and infuse for at least 20 minutes.

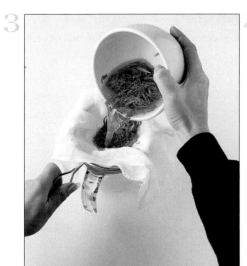

3 A sieve alone is not a sufficiently fine filter to remove all the flowers, so line it first with two layers of muslin or similar finely woven material. Pour the cooled infusion through the muslin and sieve into a clean jug or bowl. Separate 30ml (2tbs) of the marigold infusion and add a pinch of borax or other emulsifying agent such as stearic acid.

4 Cover the bottom of a pan with water and heat until nearly boiling. Put 1tbs of white beeswax in a small, heat-resistant bowl and place the bowl in the pan of hot water. Gently warm the almond oil and rose oil in the same way, transfer to a jug and pour onto the beeswax. Stir the ingredients continuously with a wooden spoon until all the beeswax has melted.

5 Gradually stir in the borax and marigold flower mixture. Mix thoroughly and continuously until it has reached an even, smooth consistency. If you are unhappy about adding a chemical to what is otherwise a completely natural recipe, omit the borax. The cream will not bind together as efficiently, however, and may need mixing before each application.

6 Remove from the heat. Allow the mixture to cool slightly. Beat in the pieces of cocoa butter with a wooden spoon. Carry on mixing the cream until it is thick and cold. Spoon into a screw-top jar. Affix a label, naming the flowers used and the date the hand cream was made. Wash the kitchen utensils in hot, soapy water to remove greasy traces of cocoa butter and beeswax.

A DROP OF
LUXURY

Floral and herbal bath oils are among the most luxurious of all bath preparations for, as well as being deliciously scented, they nourish the skin and leave it feeling silky and supple. They can be made with the minimum of effort, skill or cost, and by making your own oils, you can be absolutely sure that they contain only pure natural ingredients.

INVIGORATING PROPERTIES

Floral bath oil acts as a tonic, leaving your whole body feeling good and your skin smelling fragrant. But as well as their cosmetic uses, many flowers have specific therapeutic properties. Violets, for example, will refresh and invigorate, chamomile and rosemary will help you relax, elderflowers encourage healthy skin, and lavender eases aches and pains. When administered in the form of a bath oil, the warmth of the bath water softens the skin so that the therapeutic elements of each flower can take effect.

MAKING THE FLORAL OIL

Making floral bath oil is not too complicated but it is a lengthy procedure. It is really only a question of allowing the perfume of the fresh flowers to fuse with the oil. For best results, the flowers must be regularly replaced and the mixture strained. The oil should be left in a warm place, such as a sunny windowsill or an airing cup-

board, to absorb the flower fragrance for at least six weeks prior to use.

The best oil for making floral bath oil is untreated castor oil, also known as Turkey red oil, which is available from chemists. When mixed with the bath water it breaks down into tiny droplets and so more readily soaks into the skin while you are bathing. It is possible to use other types of oil, but they are not quite as effective. They will only float on top of the water, just settling on your skin, without being properly absorbed. Unlike untreated castor oil, other types of oil will also leave a ring around the bath after use.

A RELAXING BATH

A few drops of floral bath oil in the water is all you need, both to enjoy the fragrance and to reap the benefits of the therapeutic properties of the flowers. Do not add the oil under running hot water or it will evaporate. The temperature of the bath water is also important, a relaxing, sedative bath should be just under blood heat. If it is too hot, the skin will perspire and will not absorb the therapeutic herbal properties. Also, a very hot bath is debilitating and will dry out the skin. If you enjoy bubbles in the bath, add floral oil mixed with a tablespoon of mild liquid soap or baby shampoo. You should also keep the bathroom door and windows closed to trap in the steam so that you can inhale the

sweet-scented, therapeutic vapour of the flowers.

The best way to store the finished oil is in bottles with ground glass stoppers, away from direct light and heat. Gift shops and the glass departments of big stores stock plain and coloured glass bottles and jars in a wide range of shapes and sizes. Decorate the bottle with the appropriate flower and fasten it with a matching coloured ribbon.

SCENTED SACHETS

As a short cut to enjoying the natural fragrance of flowers in the bath, use the petals themselves without going to the trouble of blending them with oil. It is not advisable however simply to scatter petals straight into the bath, no matter how pretty they may look. They are not beneficial administered like this, and will quickly clog up the plug hole.

Rather, make a simple floral bath sachet to hold the petals. Place about three tablespoons of crushed, fresh petals, one and a half tablespoons of dried, or a mixture of the two on a piece of closely-woven washable material, such as muslin, approximately 17cm (7in) square. Gather up

Soak yourself in home-made comfort by adding perfumed lilac flower oil to a warm and relaxing bath

the corners and edges of the material around the petals. Tie the bag securely with a long piece of string, making a large loop at one end so that the bag will hang deep in the water. For a decorative finish, hide the string with a length of coloured ribbon and cover the muslin with a piece of silk or a sprigged cotton print. Hang the bag by the loop under the hot tap, so that the water and the steam mingle with the flowers, drawing out their perfume. A little oatmeal or bran mixed with the flowers will have the added benefit of making the water deliciously soft.

For a luxurious, skin-softening milk bath, add 45ml (three tablespoons) of powdered milk to the flowers in the muslin bag. Alternatively, add fresh flowers to 275ml (½ pint) of cold milk. Leave to infuse for two hours. Strain the flowers and add to a warm bath.

Floral bath sachets can be used more than once. Dry them after each bath and discard once the scent has faded.

FLOWER INFUSIONS

Another very quick and simple way of bringing the benefits of flowers to your bath is to make a strong petal infusion. For a normal-sized bath, put six tablespoons of crushed, freshly-picked petals, or three tablespoons of

1 freshly picked lilac flowers 2 castor oil 3 muslin 4 glass jar with tightly fitting lid
5 bottle with ground glass stopper 6 small tray 7 jug 8 sieve 9 saucepan
10 metal spoon

GLYCERINE BATH OIL

Rather than waiting for the scent of fresh flowers to permeate castor oil, use ready-made flower oil. Choose from one of the many available fragrances such as violet, jasmine, rose, lavender or lily of the valley. Mix about 50ml (2fl oz) of flower oil with 175ml (6fl oz) of glycerine, available from most good chemists. Store the bath oil in a sealable bottle. Give the contents a good shake before adding a few drops to a hot bath.

dried petals and one litre (1¾ pints) of water in a saucepan but do not use an aluminium one. Cover the pan and heat the mixture to just below boiling point. Remove the saucepan from the heat and leave to infuse for 20 minutes. Strain the liquid through a sieve lined with muslin, pressing down firmly on the petals to extract all their goodness.

ALTERNATIVE FLOWERS

Fresh lilac makes a delightful choice for scented bath oils, floral bath sachets and infusions but, until it starts appearing in the garden, lilac can be expensive to buy from the florist. There are many other types of flowers and herbs that make equally enjoyable alternatives. For a really refreshing pick-me-up, use eucalyptus or mint, and for an unusual spring bath tonic, use dandelion and lawn daisies from the garden. Roses, cowslips and honeysuckle also make deliciously sweet-scented bath bags.

MAKING
SWEET SCENTED LILAC BATH OIL

1 Gently remove the individual lilac flowers from the main stem. Only use flowers in perfect condition. Discard any damaged or discoloured blooms. Place each flowerhead separately on a tray. Crush each one with the back of a metal spoon so that they release their natural essence more efficiently.

2 Pack the lilac flowers tightly into a clean glass jar leaving a 2.5cm (1in) gap at the top. The more flowers that are packed into the jar, the quicker the oil will absorb the fragrance. Warm the castor oil slowly in a saucepan until it is hand hot, then pour it over the lilac until the jar is full. Fasten the lid tightly.

3 Leave the jar of flowers and oil in a warm, sunny place, such as on a windowsill, in an airing cupboard or on top of a central heating boiler for at least three weeks. Shake the contents of the jar vigorously at least once or twice daily to agitate the petals and speed up the infusion process.

4 After three weeks, when the perfume of the flowers is sufficiently mixed with the oil, remove the jar from the windowsill and gently warm it by placing it in a saucepan of water on the stove. Do not allow the mixture to boil as the flowers will spoil and the glass jar may crack.

5 Remove the lid of the jar and strain the contents through a sieve lined with muslin, or similarly closely woven material. Extract the scented oil and throw away the flowers. Repeat steps 1 to 4 two or three times, using a fresh supply of flowers each time, until the oil is well perfumed.

6 If necessary, strain the mixture through a sieve lined with two layers of muslin before pouring the finished floral oil into a glass bottle with a securely-fitting ground glass stopper. As a finishing touch, attach a pretty label to identify the fragrance of your oil.

INDEX